BUILDING RESILIENCE

Building Resilience

Nurturing Your Child's Inner Strength

DAVID OLUBIYI

Dabim Support Services Inc.

CONTENTS

This book is a comprehensive guide for parents, educators, and healthcare professionals on how to foster resilience in children and adolescents. Resilience refers to the ability to adapt and thrive in the face of adversity and challenges, and it is a crucial skill for success in all aspects of life.

The book offers practical strategies and tips for promoting resilience in children and adolescents, based on the latest research in psychology and education. It covers a wide range of topics, including emotional regulation, problem-solving, stress management, mindfulness, growth mindset, positive relationships, communication skills, and more.

Each chapter provides in-depth information and guidance on a specific topic, along with real-life examples, case studies, and practical exercises. The book also includes tips for parents and educators on how to apply these strategies in their everyday interactions with children and adolescents, as well as recommendations for additional resources and support.

Overall, this book is an essential resource for anyone who wants to help children and adolescents develop resilience and thrive in the face of challenges. It is written in a clear and accessible style, with a focus on practicality and real-world application.

HOW TO USE THIS BOOK

If you're interested in learning about fostering resilience in children and adolescents, this book can serve as a valuable resource. Here are some tips on how to use it effectively:

1. Start with an introduction: Begin by reading the introduction, which will provide an overview of what resilience is and why it's important for children and adolescents.
2. Identify your goals: Determine what you hope to gain from this book. Are you looking for strategies to help a specific child or adolescent in your life? Or are you interested in learning more about fostering resilience in general?
3. Browse the topics: Take a look at the various topics covered in the book, such as providing emotional support, setting realistic expectations, and practicing empathy. Choose the chapters that are most relevant to your goals.
4. Read with an open mind: As you read each chapter, keep an open mind and consider how the strategies and tips presented can be applied to your specific situation.
5. Take notes: As you read, take notes on the strategies and tips that you find most helpful. You may also want to jot down any questions or concerns that come up.
6. Apply what you learn: Once you've finished reading, start applying the strategies and tips you've learned to your interactions with children and adolescents. Remember that fostering resilience is an ongoing process, and it may take time to see results.

7.   Reflect and adjust: Reflect on your experiences and adjust your approach as needed. Don't be afraid to seek additional support or resources if you need them.

Overall, this book is a great starting point for anyone interested in fostering resilience in children and adolescents. By applying the strategies and tips presented, you can help the children and adolescents in your life develop the skills and abilities they need to thrive in the face of adversity.

LETTER TO PARENTS

Dear Parents,

As parents, you play a critical role in helping your children develop resilience. This is especially important in today's world, where children face a range of challenges, from academic pressures to social and emotional stressors.

This book is designed to provide you with practical strategies and tips for fostering resilience in your children. It covers a range of topics, from teaching emotional literacy to setting realistic expectations and encouraging positive relationships.

It is my hope that this book will serve as a valuable resource for you as you navigate the ups and downs of parenthood. Remember, building resilience takes time and effort, but the rewards are well worth it. By helping your children develop resilience, you are empowering them to face challenges with confidence and courage.

Thank you for taking the time to invest in your children's well-being. I wish you all the best in your journey towards building resilience in your family.

Sincerely,
David Olubiyi

TIPS FOR PARENTS

Here are some tips for parents:

1. Practice active listening: Pay attention to your child's needs and emotions, and show that you are there to support them.
2. Set realistic expectations: Encourage your child to set goals and work towards them, but also be realistic about their abilities and limitations.
3. Offer praise and positive feedback: Focus on praising effort and progress, rather than just innate abilities or intelligence.
4. Foster a growth mindset: Help your child to develop a growth mindset by emphasizing the importance of learning, encouraging mistakes, and setting challenging goals.
5. Teach emotional regulation: Help your child to identify and manage their emotions in healthy ways, such as through mindfulness and meditation.
6. Encourage social connections: Encourage your child to build positive relationships with peers, family, and community members, as social support is important for resilience.
7. Seek professional help if needed: If your child is struggling with trauma, mental health issues, or other challenges, seek the help of a mental health professional who can provide specialized support and interventions.

Remember, every child is unique and may require different strategies and support. Be patient, empathetic, and open to communication to help your child build resilience and thrive.

LETTER TO TEACHERS

I hope this letter finds you well. I am writing to express my gratitude for all that you do for our children. As educators, you have one of the most important jobs in the world – shaping the minds and futures of the next generation.

As you know, children and adolescents face many challenges in today's world. From academic pressures to social and emotional struggles, our students need all the support they can get. That's why I am excited to introduce you to my book, which is designed to provide strategies for fostering resilience in children and adolescents.

Resilience is the ability to bounce back from adversity, to adapt to change, and to grow from challenges. It is a critical skill that can help our students succeed in all areas of life. In my book, you will find practical tips and techniques for promoting resilience in your students, including:

- Teaching emotional literacy
- Encouraging positive relationships
- Developing communication skills
- Setting challenging goals
- Offering opportunities for mastery experiences
- Modeling resilience

These strategies can be incorporated into your classroom activities and can help your students to develop the skills they need to thrive.

As educators, you have a unique opportunity to make a difference in the lives of our students. By promoting resilience, you can help them to overcome challenges, build self-confidence, and achieve their goals.

Thank you for all that you do, and I look forward to continuing to work together to support the success of our students.

Sincerely,
David Olubiyi

FOREWORD

In a world filled with countless challenges and uncertainties, it is essential that we equip our children and adolescents with the tools they need to navigate life's ups and downs. "Cultivating Resilience in Children and Adolescents" is a remarkable book that offers invaluable insights and practical strategies for fostering resilience in our young ones.

In these pages, David Olubiyi takes us on a transformative journey, unveiling the power of resilience and its profound impact on the lives of children and adolescents. With a deep understanding of psychology and a genuine passion for empowering others, David presents a comprehensive guide that is both informative and inspiring.

Drawing from the latest research and his own experiences, David covers a wide range of topics, including emotional regulation, coping skills, growth mindset, positive relationships, and more. His thoughtful guidance and actionable advice make it easy for parents, educators, and healthcare professionals to implement these strategies in their daily interactions with young individuals.

What sets this book apart is David's ability to address specific challenges that children and adolescents may face, such as trauma and disabilities. His compassionate approach encourages us to create supportive environments that promote safety, security, and a sense of belonging. By emphasizing the strengths and abilities of our young ones, we empower them to overcome adversity and flourish.

As you delve into the pages of this book, be prepared to be inspired and equipped with practical tools that can truly make a difference in the lives of children and adolescents. David Olubiyi's wisdom, expertise, and passion shine through every word, making this book an indispensable resource for anyone invested in the well-being and resilience of our younger generation.

I commend David for his dedication to fostering resilience and empowering our youth. "Cultivating Resilience in Children and Adolescents" is a testament to his commitment to creating a brighter and more resilient future.

Olawumi Fasimirin
Child and Youth Support

| 1 |

Understanding Resilience

Resilience is defined as the ability to adapt and cope with stress and adversity. Resilience is not a fixed trait, but rather a set of skills that can be nurtured and strengthened over time.

Factors that contribute to resilience in children and adolescents include:

Positive Relationships

Resilience is the ability to adapt and bounce back from adversity, and it is an important trait for children and adolescents to develop. Building resilience in children and adolescents requires a multifaceted approach, and positive relationships with parents, caregivers, peers, and teachers play a crucial role. In this article, we will explore the importance of positive relationships in building resilience and provide some strategies for fostering these relationships.

Why Positive Relationships are Important for Building Resilience

Positive relationships provide children and adolescents with a sense of safety and security, and they help to build trust and confidence. Children and adolescents who have positive relationships with parents, caregivers, peers, and teachers are more likely to develop resilience because they feel supported and valued. Positive relationships also provide children and adolescents with opportunities to practice social and emotional skills, such as empathy, communication, and problem-solving, which are essential for building resilience.

Positive Relationships with Parents and Caregivers

Parents and caregivers play a crucial role in building resilience in children and adolescents. Positive relationships with parents and caregivers provide children and adolescents with a sense of belonging and security, which is essential for developing resilience. Some strategies for fostering positive relationships with parents and caregivers include:

Spending quality time together: Spending time together, such as eating meals together or engaging in activities, can help to build positive relationships and create a sense of connectedness.

Active listening: Active listening involves paying attention to what the child or adolescent is saying and showing interest in their thoughts and feelings. Active listening can help to build trust and open communication.

Expressing love and support: Expressing love and support, such as through verbal affirmations or physical affection, can help to build positive relationships and a sense of security.

Positive Relationships with Peers

Positive relationships with peers provide children and adolescents with opportunities to practice social and emotional skills, such as empathy, communication, and conflict resolution, which are essential for building resilience. Some strategies for fostering positive relationships with peers include:

Encouraging shared interests: Encouraging shared interests, such as through participation in sports or clubs, can help to build positive relationships and a sense of belonging.

Teaching conflict resolution: Teaching conflict resolution skills, such as active listening and problem-solving, can help children and adolescents to navigate social relationships and build resilience.

Modeling positive behavior: Modeling positive behavior, such as kindness and empathy, can help children and adolescents to develop these skills and build positive relationships.

Positive Relationships with Teachers: Positive relationships with teachers provide children and adolescents with opportunities to learn and grow, and they help to build trust and confidence. Some strategies for fostering positive relationships with teachers include:

Providing support and encouragement: Providing support and encouragement, such as through positive feedback and recognition, can help to build positive relationships and a sense of confidence.

Active listening: Active listening involves paying attention to what the child or adolescent is saying and showing interest in their thoughts and feelings. Active listening can help to build trust and open communication.

Creating a safe and supportive environment: Creating a safe and supportive environment, such as through clear expectations and positive reinforcement, can help to build positive relationships and a sense of security.

Positive relationships with parents, caregivers, peers, and teachers are essential for building resilience in children and adolescents. By fostering these relationships, we can help children and adolescents to feel supported and valued, develop social and emotional skills, and build trust and confidence. Building resilience is an ongoing process, and positive relationships are a crucial component of this process.

Practical scenario 1

* * *

Imagine a scenario where a child named Sarah has just started a new school. She feels nervous and uncertain about making friends and fitting in with her new classmates. However, she has a positive and supportive relationship with her mother, who regularly talks to her about her feelings and provides emotional support.

Sarah's mother encourages her to get involved in extracurricular activities, like joining the school's drama club. Through this club, Sarah is able to meet new people and form positive relationships with her fellow club members. She also develops a strong bond with her drama teacher, who recognizes her talents and provides her with encouragement and guidance.

In addition to her involvement in the drama club, Sarah also has a supportive relationship with her teacher, who takes an interest in her academic progress and provides her with extra help when needed. Through these positive relationships with her mother, drama teacher, and academic teacher, Sarah develops a sense of belonging and self-confidence. She is able to navigate the challenges of her new school and build resilience in the face of adversity.

* * *

Supportive environment

A supportive environment is a crucial element in cultivating resilience in children and adolescents. In fact, creating a supportive environment is often the foundation upon which all other resilience-building strategies are built.

A supportive environment can take many forms, but at its core, it promotes a sense of safety, security, and belonging. Children and adolescents who feel safe and secure in their environment are more likely to feel comfortable taking risks and trying new things, which are essential components of resilience.

Here are some ways in which a supportive environment can be created:

Physical safety: Ensuring that the physical environment is safe and secure is an essential element in creating a supportive environment. This can include measures such as ensuring that the home or school is free from hazards and providing appropriate supervision.

Emotional safety: Emotional safety is just as important as physical safety. A supportive environment should be one in which children and adolescents feel comfortable expressing themselves without fear of judgment or reprisal. This can be accomplished by creating an atmosphere of openness and acceptance, in which differences are celebrated and individuality is encouraged.

Consistency: A supportive environment should be consistent in terms of rules, expectations, and consequences. This consistency provides children and adolescents with a sense of predictability, which is essential for building a sense of security.

Flexibility: While consistency is important, it's also essential to be flexible and adaptable. A supportive environment should be one in which children and adolescents feel that their needs and concerns are heard and addressed, even if it means changing course or adapting to new circumstances.

Sense of belonging: A supportive environment should promote a sense of belonging and connectedness. This can be accomplished by encouraging participation in activities and events that foster a sense of community and shared experience.

By creating a supportive environment that promotes safety, security, and belonging, we can help children and adolescents to develop resilience and cope with the challenges they face in life.

Practical scenario 2

* * *

Imagine a classroom where a student named Maya has just transferred in. Maya has experienced bullying at her previous school and is nervous about making new friends. The teacher, Ms. Garcia, takes notice of Maya's nervousness and takes steps to create a supportive environment in the classroom.

First, Ms. Garcia makes sure to introduce Maya to the other students in a warm and welcoming way. She also assigns Maya a "buddy" who can show her around the school and help her get acclimated to her new environment.

Ms. Garcia also emphasizes the importance of kindness and inclusivity in the classroom. She encourages students to get to know each other, work together on projects, and share their ideas and perspectives. She also establishes a "no bullying" policy and makes it clear that any form of bullying or exclusion will not be tolerated.

To further foster a sense of safety and security, Ms. Garcia makes sure to create a predictable and consistent classroom routine. She establishes clear expectations for behavior and communicates these expectations to the students. She also provides regular feedback and positive reinforcement to encourage students to meet these expectations.

Overall, Ms. Garcia's efforts to create a supportive environment have a positive impact on Maya and the other students in the classroom. Maya feels more comfortable and confident in her new school, and the other students develop strong social connections and a sense of belonging. As a result, they are better equipped to handle challenges and setbacks, and are more likely to develop resilience.

* * *

Coping skills

Life is full of challenges and obstacles, and it's no different for children and adolescents. Whether it's academic stress, social pressures, family conflict, or other difficulties, children and adolescents face a wide range of stressors that can impact their well-being. Developing effective coping skills is essential for children and adolescents to manage stress and adversity, and to build resilience.

Coping skills refer to the strategies and techniques that individuals use to manage stress, regulate their emotions, and adapt to difficult situations. Children and adolescents who have effective coping skills are better equipped to navigate the ups and downs of life and to bounce back from setbacks. In this article, we'll explore the importance of coping skills in building resilience and discuss some effective coping strategies for children and adolescents.

The Importance of Coping Skills

Research has shown that effective coping skills are an essential component of resilience. Children and adolescents who have strong coping skills are better able to manage stress and adversity, and are more likely to experience positive outcomes in the face of adversity. Coping skills can help children and adolescents to:

Manage stress: Coping skills can help children and adolescents to manage stress and anxiety, which are common experiences in childhood and adolescence. By developing effective coping skills, children and adolescents can learn to regulate their emotions and reduce their stress levels.

Build resilience: Coping skills are an essential component of resilience, which refers to the ability to adapt and bounce back from adversity. By developing effective coping skills, children and adolescents can build their resilience and better cope with the challenges of life.

Improve mental health: Coping skills can help children and adolescents to improve their mental health and well-being. By learning effective coping strategies, children and adolescents can reduce symptoms of depression, anxiety, and other mental health conditions.

Effective Coping Strategies

There are many effective coping strategies that children and adolescents can use to manage stress and adversity. Here are some of the most effective coping strategies:

Mindfulness: Mindfulness involves paying attention to the present moment and accepting it without judgment. Mindfulness can help children and adolescents to manage stress and anxiety, and to regulate their emotions. Mindfulness techniques can include deep breathing, meditation, and visualization exercises.

Exercise: Exercise is a powerful coping strategy that can help children and adolescents to manage stress and improve their mental health. Exercise can also improve self-esteem and provide a sense of accomplishment.

Social support: Social support is a key component of resilience, and can help children and adolescents to manage stress and adversity. Having supportive friends and family members can provide a sense of comfort and belonging, and can help children and adolescents to feel less isolated.

Problem-solving: Problem-solving involves identifying a problem and coming up with a plan to solve it. By developing effective problem-solving skills, children and adolescents can better cope with difficult situations and develop a sense of control.

Relaxation techniques: Relaxation techniques can help children and adolescents to manage stress and anxiety, and to promote a sense of calm. Relaxation techniques can include deep breathing, progressive muscle relaxation, and visualization exercises.

Cognitive restructuring: Cognitive restructuring involves identifying and challenging negative thoughts and replacing them with more positive, adaptive thoughts. By developing effective cognitive restructuring skills, children and adolescents can improve their mood and reduce symptoms of depression and anxiety.

Expressive writing: Expressive writing involves writing about one's thoughts and feelings in a journal or other writing format. Expressive writing can help children and adolescents to process difficult emotions and develop a sense of clarity and perspective.

Developing effective coping skills is essential for children and adolescents to manage stress and adversity, and to build resilience. Coping skills can help children and adolescents to manage stress, regulate their emotions, and adapt to difficult situations. By developing effective coping strategies such as

---

Practical scenario 3
***

Emma is a 12-year-old girl who is going through a difficult time at school. She has been struggling with her grades and has been having a hard time making friends. Emma is feeling overwhelmed and anxious, and is having trouble sleeping at night.

Emma's parents have noticed that she has been struggling and have decided to seek help from a therapist. The therapist works with Emma to develop coping skills to help her manage her stress and anxiety.

The therapist teaches Emma deep breathing exercises, which she can use when she feels overwhelmed. Emma also learns how to identify her negative thoughts and replace them with more positive ones. Additionally, the therapist works with Emma to develop a self-care plan that includes exercise, healthy eating, and getting enough sleep.

Over time, Emma starts to feel more in control of her thoughts and emotions. She is able to use her coping skills to manage her stress and anxiety, and feels more confident in herself. Emma's grades improve, and she starts to make friends at school.

Thanks to the coping skills she learned, Emma is better equipped to handle future challenges and has developed a sense of resilience.

***

Growth mindset

A growth mindset is an important concept that can help children and adolescents develop resilience. It emphasizes the importance of effort and persistence in learning, and can help children and adolescents to view challenges as opportunities for growth and learning. In this article, we'll explore the importance of a growth mindset in developing resilience and discuss some strategies for cultivating a growth mindset in children and adolescents.

What is a Growth Mindset?

A growth mindset is the belief that abilities and intelligence can be developed through hard work, dedication, and persistence. People with a growth mindset believe that they can improve and develop their skills and abilities over time, and they view challenges and failures as opportunities for growth and learning.

In contrast, a fixed mindset is the belief that abilities and intelligence are fixed traits that cannot be changed. People with a fixed mindset tend to avoid challenges and give up easily when faced with obstacles, as they believe that their abilities are predetermined.

The Importance of a Growth Mindset in Developing Resilience

Research has shown that a growth mindset can help children and adolescents develop resilience by providing them with the tools they need to overcome challenges and setbacks. Here are some of the ways in which a growth mindset can help children and adolescents to develop resilience:

Embracing challenges: Children and adolescents with a growth mindset view challenges as opportunities for growth and learning, rather than as threats to their abilities. This can help them to approach challenges with a sense of curiosity and excitement, rather than with fear or avoidance.

Persistence and effort: Children and adolescents with a growth mindset understand that success is not just about innate abilities, but also about persistence and effort. This can help them to persist in the face of challenges and setbacks, and to work hard to achieve their goals.

Learning from failure: Children and adolescents with a growth mindset view failure as a natural part of the learning process. They understand that failure is an opportunity to learn from their mistakes and to improve their skills and abilities.

Self-efficacy: Children and adolescents with a growth mindset have a strong sense of self-efficacy, or belief in their ability to succeed. This can help them to approach challenges with confidence and to persevere in the face of adversity.

Resilience: Children and adolescents with a growth mindset are better equipped to bounce back from setbacks and to develop resilience. They understand that setbacks are not permanent, and that they can continue to learn and grow even in the face of adversity.

Strategies for Cultivating a Growth Mindset in Children and Adolescents

Here are some strategies for cultivating a growth mindset in children and adolescents:

Encourage effort: Encourage children and adolescents to focus on effort and persistence, rather than just outcomes. Praise them for their hard work and dedication, rather than just their achievements.

Model a growth mindset: Model a growth mindset by embracing challenges, persisting in the face of setbacks, and learning from failure. Let children and adolescents see you work hard to achieve your goals, and talk to them about the importance of effort and persistence.

Use growth mindset language: Use language that emphasizes effort and growth, rather than fixed abilities. Encourage children and adolescents to use language such as "I can't do it yet," rather than "I can't do it."

Provide opportunities for growth: Provide children and adolescents with opportunities to learn and grow, such as trying new activities, taking on challenges, and learning new skills.

Celebrate mistakes: Celebrate mistakes and use them as opportunities for learning and growth. Encourage children and adolescents to view mistakes as natural parts of the learning process, rather than as signs of failure.

A growth mindset is an important concept that can help children and adolescents to develop resilience. By emphasizing the importance of effort and persistence,

A Scenario on growth mindset

Practical scenario 4
✴ ✴ ✴

Samantha is a 10-year-old student who loves playing the violin. She has been taking lessons for a year, but she still struggles with some of the more difficult pieces. One day, her music teacher assigns a new piece that Samantha finds especially challenging. She practices diligently for a week, but still can't seem to get the notes quite right. She begins to feel frustrated and discouraged, thinking that maybe she's just not good enough at playing the violin.

Samantha's music teacher notices her struggling and sits down with her for a conversation. She explains to Samantha that everyone struggles with learning new things, and that making mistakes is a natural part of the learning process. She encourages Samantha to adopt a growth mindset, which means focusing on the effort she is putting in rather than the immediate results. The teacher tells Samantha that the fact that she is practicing so hard and trying to learn the new piece is already a sign of progress and growth, and that with time and practice, she will get better and better.

Samantha takes the teacher's words to heart and begins to approach the new piece with a new perspective. Instead of getting discouraged by her mistakes, she sees them as opportunities to learn and improve. She starts practicing even more diligently, focusing on the parts that she finds difficult and asking her teacher for feedback. Gradually, she begins to make progress and feel more confident in her ability to play the piece.

By adopting a growth mindset, Samantha was able to overcome her initial feelings of discouragement and frustration, and turn her struggle into an opportunity for growth and learning. She learned to focus on the effort she was putting in rather than the immediate results, and to see mistakes as opportunities for improvement. These skills will serve her well not just in playing the violin, but in all areas of her life.

* * *

Promoting Self-Efficacy

Self-efficacy is a person's belief in their ability to overcome challenges and achieve their goals. This belief is an important factor in resilience, as it helps individuals to persist in the face of adversity and bounce back from setbacks. In this article, we'll explore the concept of self-efficacy and its role in developing resilience, and discuss some strategies for cultivating self-efficacy in children and adolescents.

What is Self-Efficacy?

Self-efficacy is a person's belief in their ability to successfully complete tasks, overcome challenges, and achieve their goals. It is a key component of Bandura's social-cognitive theory, which posits that self-efficacy is a major determinant of behavior and motivation.

Self-efficacy is influenced by a variety of factors, including past experiences, social and cultural contexts, and individual characteristics such as personality and temperament. People with high self-efficacy tend to approach challenges with confidence, view failures as opportunities for learning and growth, and persist in the face of adversity.

The Role of Self-Efficacy in Developing Resilience:

Self-efficacy plays a crucial role in developing resilience, as it helps individuals to bounce back from setbacks and persevere in the face of adversity. Here are some ways in which self-efficacy contributes to resilience:

Persistence: People with high self-efficacy tend to persist in the face of obstacles and setbacks, as they believe that they have the ability to overcome challenges and achieve their goals.

Coping with stress: People with high self-efficacy are better able to cope with stress and adversity, as they believe that they have the skills and resources necessary to manage difficult situations.

Motivation: Self-efficacy is a key component of motivation, as people with high self-efficacy are more likely to set challenging goals and work hard to achieve them.

Adaptability: People with high self-efficacy are more adaptable to changing circumstances, as they are confident in their ability to handle new challenges and unfamiliar situations.

Cultivating Self-Efficacy in Children and Adolescents:

Here are some strategies for cultivating self-efficacy in children and adolescents:

Encourage Mastery Experiences: Encourage children and adolescents to engage in activities that allow them to experience success and mastery. Provide opportunities for them to develop new skills and challenge themselves in a supportive environment.

Provide Positive Feedback: Provide positive and specific feedback that acknowledges and reinforces their accomplishments. This can help to build their confidence and reinforce their belief in their ability to succeed.

Model Resilient Behavior: Model resilient behavior by demonstrating perseverance and persistence in the face of challenges. Talk openly with children and adolescents about your own experiences with setbacks and how you overcame them.

Encourage Positive Self-Talk: Encourage children and adolescents to use positive self-talk, such as affirmations or motivational statements, to reinforce their belief in their ability to succeed.

Promote Goal-Setting: Encourage children and adolescents to set challenging but achievable goals and provide them with the support they need to achieve them. This can help to build their confidence and reinforce their belief in their ability to succeed.

Self-efficacy is a critical component of resilience, as it helps individuals to persist in the face of adversity and bounce back from setbacks. Cultivating self-efficacy in children and adolescents can help to build their confidence, motivation, and adaptability, and prepare them to face the challenges of life with resilience and determination. By providing opportunities for mastery experiences, positive feedback, and goal-setting, parents and caregivers can help children and adolescents develop the self-efficacy they need to thrive.

Practical scenario 5
* * *

Imagine a student, Sarah, who has always struggled with math. She has had a difficult time keeping up with her classmates and often feels discouraged and frustrated. However, her teacher notices that when given challenging math problems, Sarah is willing to try and persists until she figures it out.

The teacher recognizes this as a sign of self-efficacy, or Sarah's belief in her ability to succeed despite her struggles. The teacher then starts to give Sarah more challenging math problems and provides her with additional support and resources to help her succeed.

As a result, Sarah's self-efficacy continues to grow. She begins to believe that she can overcome her struggles in math and achieve her academic goals. Over time, she becomes more confident and motivated to take on other challenges in school and in her personal life. Sarah's resilience has grown through her belief in her own abilities to succeed.

* * *

Developing Social and Emotional Intelligence

Resilience is the ability to adapt and bounce back in the face of adversity. While there are many factors that contribute to resilience, social and emotional intelligence play a critical role in helping children and adolescents to cope with difficult situations. In this article, we'll explore the concept of social and emotional intelligence and its role in developing resilience, and discuss some strategies for cultivating social and emotional intelligence in children and adolescents.

What is Social and Emotional Intelligence?

Social and emotional intelligence refers to the ability to understand and manage emotions, and to navigate social relationships effectively. It involves a range of skills, including self-awareness, self-regulation, empathy, and social skills.

Self-awareness: Self-awareness is the ability to recognize and understand one's own emotions, thoughts, and behaviors. People with high levels of self-awareness are better able to regulate their emotions and manage stress.

Self-regulation: Self-regulation is the ability to manage one's own emotions and behavior. It involves the ability to control impulses, manage stress, and stay focused on goals.

Empathy: Empathy is the ability to understand and share the feelings of others. People with high levels of empathy are better able to build positive relationships and navigate social situations effectively.

Social skills: Social skills are the ability to communicate effectively, build positive relationships, and navigate social situations. People with high levels of social skills are better able to work in teams, negotiate, and resolve conflicts.

The Role of Social and Emotional Intelligence in Developing Resilience:

Social and emotional intelligence play a critical role in developing resilience, as they help children and adolescents to cope with difficult situations and build positive relationships. Here are some ways in which social and emotional intelligence contribute to resilience:

Coping with stress: People with high levels of social and emotional intelligence are better able to manage stress and cope with difficult situations, as they have the skills and strategies necessary to regulate their emotions and stay focused on their goals.

Building positive relationships: Social and emotional intelligence are essential for building positive relationships with peers, caregivers, and teachers. Positive relationships provide children and adolescents with a sense of support and belonging, which is critical for developing resilience.

Navigating social situations: Social and emotional intelligence are essential for navigating social situations effectively. Children and adolescents with high levels of social and emotional intelligence are better able to communicate effectively, resolve conflicts, and build positive relationships.

Developing self-awareness: Self-awareness is critical for developing resilience, as it helps children and adolescents to recognize their emotions and regulate their behavior effectively. Children and adolescents with high levels of self-awareness are better able to cope with difficult situations and bounce back from setbacks.

Cultivating Social and Emotional Intelligence in Children and Adolescents:

Here are some strategies for cultivating social and emotional intelligence in children and adolescents:

Encourage emotional expression: Encourage children and adolescents to express their emotions in healthy ways, such as through journaling, talking with a trusted adult, or engaging in physical activity.

Teach emotional regulation: Teach children and adolescents strategies for regulating their emotions, such as deep breathing, mindfulness, or visualization.

Model empathy: Model empathy by demonstrating compassion and understanding towards others. Talk openly with children and adolescents about the feelings of others and how to respond to them in a positive way.

Promote social skills: Provide opportunities for children and adolescents to develop social skills, such as through team sports, clubs, or volunteering. Encourage them to practice communication and conflict resolution skills.

Encourage self-reflection: Encourage children and adolescents to reflect on their emotions, thoughts, and behaviors, and to identify areas where they can improve their social and emotional intelligence.

Social and emotional intelligence play a critical role in developing resilience, as they help children and adolescents

Practical scenario 6
* * *

Samantha is a 14-year-old girl who recently started high school. She's always been a bit shy and anxious in social situations, but she's been especially struggling with the transition to high school. Samantha feels like she doesn't fit in with her peers and often worries about what others think of her. She's also been having trouble managing her emotions, and has noticed that she gets upset and anxious more easily than she used to.

Samantha's school offers a social and emotional learning program that teaches students coping skills, emotional regulation, and social skills. She decides to sign up for the program and attends weekly group sessions with other students who are also struggling with similar issues.

Through the program, Samantha learns different coping skills, such as deep breathing and positive self-talk, which she can use when she feels anxious or upset. She also learns about emotional regulation and how to identify and express her feelings in a healthy way. Samantha discovers that other students in the program are experiencing similar struggles, and she feels less alone and more understood.

In addition, Samantha learns social skills such as active listening, effective communication, and problem-solving. She practices these skills in group activities and discussions, which helps her feel more confident in social situations. Samantha even makes a few new friends in the program, and feels like she has a supportive community to turn to.

Overall, the social and emotional learning program helps Samantha develop her social and emotional intelligence, which in turn strengthens her resilience. She feels more equipped to navigate the challenges of high school and feels more confident in herself and her abilities.

* * *

| 2 |

Building a Foundation for Resilience

Positive relationships and a supportive environment are critical components in building resilience. Strategies for fostering positive relationships between children and their caregivers, peers, and teachers include:

Building trust and rapport

Building trust and rapport with children and adolescents is essential for promoting resilience. When children and adolescents feel supported, understood, and valued by the adults in their lives, they are more likely to develop the skills and qualities necessary to cope with adversity. In this article, we'll explore the importance of building trust and rapport with children and adolescents, and discuss some strategies for doing so.

Why is Building Trust and Rapport Important?

Building trust and rapport with children and adolescents is important for several reasons:

It promotes a sense of safety and security: When children and adolescents feel that the adults in their lives are trustworthy and reliable, they are more likely to feel safe and secure. This sense of safety and security is essential for promoting resilience, as it allows children and adolescents to feel that they have a secure base from which to explore and take risks.

It fosters positive relationships: Building trust and rapport with children and adolescents is essential for fostering positive relationships. Positive relationships provide children and adolescents with a sense of support and belonging, which is critical for developing resilience.

It promotes open communication: When children and adolescents trust the adults in their lives, they are more likely to communicate openly and honestly. This open communication is essential for promoting resilience, as it allows children and adolescents to express their thoughts and feelings and seek help when needed.

Strategies for Building Trust and Rapport with Children and Adolescents:

Here are some strategies for building trust and rapport with children and adolescents:

Listen actively: When children and adolescents feel that they are being listened to and understood, they are more likely to trust the adults in their lives. Practice active listening by giving your full attention, repeating back what you've heard, and asking clarifying questions.

Show empathy: Demonstrate empathy by acknowledging and validating the feelings of children and adolescents. Let them know that you understand how they feel and that you are there to support them.

Be consistent: Consistency is key to building trust and rapport with children and adolescents. Be consistent in your actions, words, and behavior, and follow through on your commitments.

Respect boundaries: Respect the boundaries of children and adolescents by not overstepping or invading their personal space. Let them set the pace for building trust and rapport, and be patient.

Provide positive feedback: Provide children and adolescents with positive feedback and praise when they demonstrate positive behavior. This positive reinforcement helps to build trust and rapport and encourages children and adolescents to continue demonstrating positive behavior.

Be approachable: Be approachable and accessible to children and adolescents. Let them know that you are available to talk and that you care about their well-being.

Building trust and rapport with children and adolescents is essential for promoting resilience. When children and adolescents feel supported, understood, and valued by the adults in their lives, they are more likely to develop the skills and qualities necessary to cope with adversity. By listening actively, showing empathy, being consistent, respecting boundaries, providing positive feedback, and being approachable, you can build trust and rapport with children and adolescents and promote their resilience.

Scenario 7

* * *

Mrs. Johnson is a new teacher at a middle school, and she has a student in her class named Alex who has a history of behavioral issues and low academic performance. On the first day of class, Mrs. Johnson notices that Alex seems disinterested and disengaged, and he is not participating in class activities.

Mrs. Johnson decides to take some time to build trust and rapport with Alex. She begins by having one-on-one meetings with him to get to know him better and understand his interests and challenges. During these meetings, Mrs. Johnson listens attentively to Alex and validates his feelings and experiences.

Mrs. Johnson also makes an effort to praise Alex for his strengths and efforts in class, rather than focusing on his past mistakes. She provides him with opportunities for success, such as giving him small tasks to complete in class and acknowledging his progress.

Over time, Mrs. Johnson's efforts pay off, and Alex begins to feel more comfortable and engaged in class. He starts participating in activities and asking questions, and his grades improve. Mrs. Johnson continues to support and encourage Alex, and he becomes one of the most enthusiastic and successful students in the class.

Through her efforts to build trust and rapport with Alex, Mrs. Johnson helped him to develop resilience and confidence in his abilities. She showed him that she cared about his success and believed in his potential, which motivated him to work harder and overcome his past challenges.

* * *

Active listening

Active listening is an essential skill for building trust and rapport with children and adolescents, as it helps them feel heard, validated, and understood. When adults practice active listening with children and adolescents, they are better able to establish positive relationships and promote resilience. In this article, we'll explore the importance of active listening, and provide some strategies for practicing it with children and adolescents.

Why is Active Listening Important?

Active listening is important for several reasons:

It shows that you care: When you listen actively to children and adolescents, you demonstrate that you care about what they have to say. This can help them feel valued and respected, which is critical for building trust and rapport.

It promotes open communication: Active listening promotes open communication by encouraging children and adolescents to share their thoughts, feelings, and experiences. This can help adults understand the challenges that children and adolescents are facing and provide them with appropriate support.

It validates feelings: Active listening validates the feelings of children and adolescents by acknowledging their emotions and demonstrating empathy. This can help children and adolescents feel heard and understood, which is critical for promoting resilience.

Strategies for Practicing Active Listening with Children and Adolescents:

Here are some strategies for practicing active listening with children and adolescents:

Give your full attention: When you are listening to a child or adolescent, give them your full attention. Put away distractions such as your phone or computer, and focus on what they are saying.

Use open-ended questions: Use open-ended questions to encourage children and adolescents to share more information. For example, instead of asking, "Did you have a good day at school?" try asking, "What was the best part of your day?"

Paraphrase what you hear: Paraphrasing what you hear can help you ensure that you are understanding the child or adolescent correctly. It can also help the child or adolescent feel heard and understood. For example, you might say, "So what I'm hearing is that you're feeling frustrated because your friend didn't invite you to their birthday party?"

Show empathy: Show empathy by acknowledging the child or adolescent's feelings and demonstrating that you understand how they feel. For example, you might say, "It sounds like you're feeling really disappointed about not being invited to the party. I can understand why that would be hard for you."

Validate feelings: Validate the child or adolescent's feelings by acknowledging that it's okay to feel the way they do. For example, you might say, "It's okay to feel sad about not being invited to the party. Anyone would feel that way."

Active listening is an essential skill for building trust and rapport with children and adolescents. When adults practice active listening with children and adolescents, they demonstrate that they care, promote open communication, and validate feelings. By giving your full attention, using open-ended questions, paraphrasing what you hear, showing empathy, and validating feelings, you can practice active listening with children and adolescents and promote their resilience.

Scenario 8

* * *

A 12-year-old girl named Lily comes home from school and looks upset. Her mother notices this and asks her what's wrong. Lily begins to tell her about a disagreement she had with her best friend, Emily, earlier that day.

As Lily talks, her mother listens attentively, making eye contact and nodding in understanding. She occasionally asks clarifying questions to ensure she understands Lily's perspective. As Lily finishes, her mother validates her feelings, saying, "It sounds like that was really hurtful, and I can understand why you're upset."

Lily's mother then asks if she would like to talk more about it or if there's anything she can do to help. Lily thanks her mother for listening and decides to spend some time alone in her room to process her emotions.

By actively listening to Lily, her mother demonstrated that she cared about her feelings and valued her perspective. This helped Lily feel

> heard and validated, which can go a long way in promoting emotional well-being and resilience.
>
> * * *

Providing emotional support

Emotional support is an essential aspect of promoting resilience in children and adolescents. When adults provide emotional support to children and adolescents, they are better able to cope with stress and adversity. In this article, we will explore the importance of emotional support, and provide some strategies for providing it to children and adolescents.

Why is Emotional Support Important?

Emotional support is important for several reasons:

It promotes resilience: Emotional support promotes resilience by helping children and adolescents cope with stress and adversity. When children and adolescents feel supported, they are better able to manage difficult situations and bounce back from setbacks.

It builds trust and rapport: Emotional support helps to build trust and rapport between adults and children or adolescents. When adults provide emotional support, they demonstrate that they care about the child or adolescent, which can help to establish a positive relationship.

It fosters emotional intelligence: Emotional support fosters emotional intelligence by helping children and adolescents to identify and manage their emotions. When adults provide emotional support, they model healthy emotional expression and provide guidance on how to cope with difficult emotions.

Strategies for Providing Emotional Support:

Here are some strategies for providing emotional support to children and adolescents:

Practice empathy: Empathy is the ability to understand and share the feelings of others. When you practice empathy with children and adolescents, you demonstrate that you care about their experiences and feelings. You can show empathy by actively listening to their concerns, acknowledging their emotions, and validating their experiences.

Encourage healthy coping mechanisms: Encourage children and adolescents to develop healthy coping mechanisms for managing stress and adversity. This might include engaging in physical activity, practicing mindfulness, or talking to a trusted adult.

Provide encouragement: Provide encouragement by acknowledging the child or adolescent's efforts and progress. For example, you might say, "I'm proud of you for working so hard on that project" or "You're doing a great job managing your stress."

Foster a positive environment: Foster a positive environment by providing opportunities for positive reinforcement and recognition. This might include celebrating achievements, providing positive feedback, or creating a supportive community.

Model healthy emotional expression: Model healthy emotional expression by expressing your own emotions in a healthy and constructive way. For example, you might say, "I'm feeling frustrated right now, but I'm going to take some deep breaths and try to calm down."

Emotional support is an essential aspect of promoting resilience in children and adolescents. When adults provide emotional support, they promote resilience, build trust and rapport, and foster emotional intelligence. By practicing empathy, encouraging healthy coping mechanisms, providing encouragement, fostering a positive environment, and modeling healthy emotional expression, you can provide emotional support to children and adolescents and help them develop resilience.

Scenario 9

***

Sophie, a 12-year-old student, has been struggling with her math class. She often feels frustrated and overwhelmed, which affects her confidence and motivation to learn. Sophie's teacher notices her struggle and decides to provide emotional support to help her feel more resilient.

One day after class, Sophie's teacher invites her to talk and listens attentively as Sophie shares her difficulties in math class. The teacher provides emotional support by acknowledging Sophie's feelings and offering words of encouragement. The teacher also empathizes with Sophie, sharing their own experience of struggling with a subject in school and how they overcame it.

The teacher suggests that Sophie can come for extra help after school or seek support from a tutor to improve her math skills. The teacher also praises Sophie's efforts and reminds her of her other strengths and abilities outside of math.

Sophie feels validated and supported by her teacher's emotional support. She realizes that she is not alone in her struggles and feels more motivated to seek help and improve her math skills. Sophie also feels more confident in her abilities overall, knowing that she has a supportive teacher who cares about her well-being.

***

Setting realistic expectations

Setting realistic expectations is an important factor in promoting resilience in children and adolescents. When children and adolescents have a sense of competence and mastery, they are better able to manage stress and adversity. In this article, we will explore the importance of setting realistic expectations, and provide some strategies for doing so.

Why is Setting Realistic Expectations Important?

Setting realistic expectations is important for several reasons:

It promotes competence and mastery: Setting realistic expectations helps children and adolescents develop a sense of competence and mastery. When expectations are too high or unrealistic, children and adolescents may feel overwhelmed, anxious, or defeated.

It fosters self-esteem: Setting realistic expectations can help children and adolescents develop self-esteem by providing opportunities for success and achievement. When children and adolescents meet realistic expectations, they feel a sense of accomplishment and pride.

It encourages growth: Setting realistic expectations encourages growth by providing opportunities for learning and improvement. When children and adolescents are challenged to meet realistic expectations, they are motivated to develop new skills and abilities.

Strategies for Setting Realistic Expectations:

Here are some strategies for setting realistic expectations for children and adolescents:

Be specific: When setting expectations, be specific about what is expected. This might include specific behaviors, actions, or outcomes. For example, instead of saying "Do your best," you might say, "Complete the task by Friday and include at least three sources."

Consider individual needs: Consider the individual needs and abilities of the child or adolescent when setting expectations. Some children and adolescents may need more support or guidance than others.

Provide feedback: Provide feedback on progress towards meeting expectations. This can help children and adolescents understand where they need to improve and where they are doing well.

Break tasks into manageable parts: When setting expectations for larger tasks or projects, break them into smaller, more manageable parts. This can help children and adolescents feel less overwhelmed and more confident in their ability to meet expectations.

Adjust expectations as needed: Be willing to adjust expectations as needed. If a child or adolescent is struggling to meet expectations, consider adjusting them to better fit their abilities or needs.

Setting realistic expectations is an important factor in promoting resilience in children and adolescents. When expectations are realistic, children and adolescents develop a sense of competence and mastery, foster self-esteem, and are encouraged to grow and learn. By being specific, considering individual needs, providing feedback, breaking tasks into manageable parts, and adjusting expectations as needed, you can set realistic expectations for children and adolescents and help them develop resilience.

Scenario 10

* * *

Maria is a high school student who has always struggled with math. She often feels frustrated and discouraged when she doesn't understand a concept or doesn't do well on an exam. Her parents have high expectations for her to excel in school and often push her to take advanced math courses.

Maria's math teacher recognizes her struggles and suggests that she meets with a tutor after school. The tutor works with Maria to identify her strengths and weaknesses in math and creates a personalized study plan for her. The tutor also emphasizes the importance of setting realistic goals and expectations.

With the tutor's help, Maria begins to see small improvements in her math skills. She no longer feels overwhelmed by the material and has more confidence in her abilities. The tutor encourages her to focus on her progress rather than comparing herself to others.

Over time, Maria sets realistic goals for herself and celebrates her successes along the way. She no longer feels the pressure to meet her parents' high expectations and instead focuses on her own growth and development. By setting realistic expectations and emphasizing progress over perfection, Maria develops a sense of competence and mastery in math.

* * *

Offering praise and positive feedback

Offering praise and positive feedback is an important factor in promoting resilience in children and adolescents. Praising children and adolescents for their efforts, rather than their innate abilities, can help them to develop a growth mindset. In this article, we will explore the importance of offering praise and positive feedback, and provide some strategies for doing so.

Why is Offering Praise and Positive Feedback Important?

Offering praise and positive feedback is important for several reasons:

It promotes a growth mindset: Praising children and adolescents for their efforts, rather than their innate abilities, can help them develop a growth mindset. A growth mindset emphasizes the importance of effort and persistence in learning, rather than innate abilities.

It fosters self-esteem: Offering praise and positive feedback can help children and adolescents develop self-esteem by providing opportunities for success and achievement. When children and adolescents receive praise for their efforts, they feel a sense of accomplishment and pride.

It strengthens relationships: Offering praise and positive feedback can help to strengthen relationships between children and adolescents and the adults in their lives. When children and adolescents feel valued and appreciated, they are more likely to form positive relationships with others.

Strategies for Offering Praise and Positive Feedback:

Here are some strategies for offering praise and positive feedback for children and adolescents:

Be specific: When offering praise and positive feedback, be specific about what the child or adolescent did well. This might include specific behaviors, actions, or outcomes. For example, instead of saying "Good job," you might say "I really appreciate the effort you put into that project. Your research was thorough, and your presentation was well-organized."

Focus on effort: When offering praise and positive feedback, focus on the child or adolescent's efforts, rather than their innate abilities. For example, instead of saying "You're so smart," you might say "I'm impressed with the effort you put into that task. You worked hard and it really paid off."

Use "and" instead of "but": When offering feedback, use "and" instead of "but" to connect positive and negative aspects. For example, instead of saying "You did a good job, but you could have done better," you might say "You did a good job, and with a little more effort, you can do even better next time."

Offer praise for progress, not just achievement: Offer praise and positive feedback for progress towards goals, not just achievement. This can help children and adolescents feel motivated to continue making progress, even if they have not yet achieved their goals.

Be sincere: When offering praise and positive feedback, be sincere. Children and adolescents can usually tell when praise is insincere, which can undermine their confidence and trust.

Offering praise and positive feedback is an important factor in promoting resilience in children and adolescents. When children and adolescents receive praise for their efforts, rather than their innate abilities, they develop a growth mindset, foster self-esteem, and form positive relationships with others. By being specific, focusing on effort, using "and" instead of "but," offering praise for progress, and being sincere, you can offer effective praise and positive feedback for children and adolescents and help them develop resilience.

Scenario 11

* * *

Imagine a young girl named Lily who is struggling with math in school. Despite putting in effort and attending extra help sessions, she still finds it difficult to understand some of the concepts. Her teacher notices her efforts and progress and decides to provide praise and positive feedback to encourage her to continue.

Instead of simply saying "good job," the teacher says something like, "I can see that you've been working really hard on your math skills. I am impressed with your perseverance and the progress you've made. Keep up the great work!"

Upon hearing this, Lily feels encouraged and motivated to continue putting in effort and working on her math skills. She begins to see her struggles as an opportunity for growth and improvement, rather than a fixed ability that she cannot change.

Over time, Lily's confidence and ability in math improve, and she begins to see herself as capable and competent in this subject. This shift in mindset and belief in her own abilities is a result of the teacher's intentional praise and positive feedback, which helped to develop a growth mindset within Lily.

* * *

| 3 |

Teaching Coping Skills

Effective coping skills are essential for developing resilience. Strategies for teaching coping skills to children and adolescents include:

Identifying and managing emotions

Emotions play an important role in our lives, influencing our thoughts, behaviors, and overall well-being. Helping children and adolescents to identify and manage their emotions is crucial for promoting resilience. When children and adolescents can effectively identify and manage their emotions, they are better able to regulate their emotional responses to stress and adversity. In this article, we will explore the importance of identifying and managing emotions, and provide some strategies for helping children and adolescents to do so.

Why is Identifying and Managing Emotions Important?

Identifying and managing emotions is important for several reasons:

It promotes emotional regulation: Emotional regulation refers to the ability to manage and control one's emotions. When children and adolescents can effectively identify and manage their emotions, they are better able to regulate their emotional responses to stress and adversity.

It fosters self-awareness: Identifying and managing emotions requires self-awareness. When children and adolescents are aware of their emotions, they are better able to understand their own needs and feelings.

It strengthens relationships: When children and adolescents can effectively identify and manage their emotions, they are better able to communicate their feelings to others. This can help to strengthen relationships between children and adolescents and the adults in their lives.

Strategies for Identifying and Managing Emotions:

Here are some strategies for helping children and adolescents to identify and manage their emotions:

Teach emotional vocabulary: Help children and adolescents to identify and name their emotions by teaching them emotional vocabulary. This can include basic emotions like happiness, sadness, anger, fear, and disgust, as well as more complex emotions like jealousy, embarrassment, and pride.

Practice mindfulness: Mindfulness involves paying attention to the present moment, without judgment. Practicing mindfulness can help children and adolescents to become more aware of their emotions and to regulate their emotional responses. Mindfulness exercises can include deep breathing, body scans, and meditation.

Encourage emotional expression: Encourage children and adolescents to express their emotions in a healthy way. This might include talking about their feelings, writing in a journal, or engaging in creative activities like art or music.

Model healthy emotional expression: Model healthy emotional expression by expressing your own emotions in a healthy way. This might include talking about your feelings with your child or adolescent, or modeling healthy coping strategies like deep breathing or taking a break when feeling overwhelmed.

Practice problem-solving: Help children and adolescents to identify and solve problems that are causing negative emotions. This might include brainstorming solutions, weighing pros and cons, and developing a plan of action.

Identifying and managing emotions is an important factor in promoting resilience in children and adolescents. By teaching emotional vocabulary, practicing mindfulness, encouraging emotional expression, modeling healthy emotional expression, and practicing problem-solving, you can help children and adolescents to effectively identify and manage their emotions. When children and adolescents can effectively identify and manage their emotions, they are better able to regulate their emotional responses to stress and adversity, foster self-awareness, and strengthen relationships with others.

Problem-solving

Problem-solving is an essential skill that children and adolescents need to develop in order to navigate the challenges they will face in life. By teaching children and adolescents problem-solving skills, they can learn how to identify and address challenges effectively, and develop the resilience needed to overcome obstacles. In this article, we will explore the importance of problem-solving and provide some strategies for teaching children and adolescents problem-solving skills.

Why is Problem-Solving Important?

Problem-solving is important for several reasons:

It promotes independence: When children and adolescents learn how to solve problems on their own, they become more independent and self-reliant.

It fosters creativity: Problem-solving requires creativity and innovation. When children and adolescents learn how to solve problems, they become more creative and resourceful.

It develops resilience: Problem-solving helps children and adolescents to develop resilience by teaching them how to overcome obstacles and challenges.

Strategies for Teaching Problem-Solving Skills:

Here are some strategies for teaching problem-solving skills to children and adolescents:

Encourage critical thinking: Encourage children and adolescents to think critically by asking open-ended questions that require them to consider different perspectives and options.

Teach the problem-solving process: Teach children and adolescents the problem-solving process, which involves identifying the problem, brainstorming solutions, selecting the best solution, and implementing it.

Model problem-solving: Model problem-solving by demonstrating how you approach challenges and obstacles in your own life. This can help children and adolescents to learn how to solve problems effectively.

Encourage collaboration: Encourage children and adolescents to work together to solve problems, as this can help to develop teamwork skills and foster creativity.

Provide opportunities for practice: Provide children and adolescents with opportunities to practice problem-solving skills in real-life situations, such as through role-playing or simulations.

Teaching problem-solving skills to children and adolescents is an important part of promoting resilience. By encouraging critical thinking, teaching the problem-solving process, modeling problem-solving, encouraging collaboration, and providing opportunities for practice, you can help children and adolescents to develop the skills they need to identify and address challenges effectively. When children and adolescents develop problem-solving skills, they become more independent, creative, and resilient, which will help them to navigate the challenges they will face in life.

Scenario 12

* * *

Mark is a 12-year-old student who is struggling with math. He is finding it difficult to understand fractions, which is affecting his performance in class. He is becoming increasingly frustrated and discouraged and is starting to believe that he is not good at math.

Mark's teacher recognizes that he is struggling and decides to teach him problem-solving skills to help him address his difficulties with fractions. The teacher uses a problem-solving model that involves the following steps:

Identify the problem: Mark and his teacher discuss the issue he is having with fractions, and they identify that he is struggling to understand the concept.

Brainstorm possible solutions: Mark and his teacher brainstorm possible solutions to the problem. They come up with several options, such as asking for extra help, practicing more, or finding online resources to help with understanding fractions.

Evaluate the solutions: Mark and his teacher evaluate each of the possible solutions based on how effective they might be and how feasible they are to implement. They determine that practicing more and seeking extra help are the most effective and feasible solutions.

Choose the best solution: Based on the evaluation, Mark and his teacher decide that practicing more and seeking extra help are the best solutions to address his difficulties with fractions.

Implement the solution: Mark starts practicing more and seeking extra help from his teacher and peers. He attends after-school math sessions and works on fractions during his free time.

Evaluate the outcome: After implementing the solutions, Mark's teacher evaluates his progress. She observes that Mark is improving his understanding of fractions and is performing better in class. She also notices that he is becoming more confident in his math abilities and is motivated to continue working on his math skills.

Through this problem-solving model, Mark is able to identify and address his difficulties with fractions effectively. He develops a sense of competence and mastery as he works through the problem-solving process, which helps to build his resilience and confidence.

* * *

Stress management

Stress and anxiety are common experiences for children and adolescents, and can have a significant impact on their mental health and wellbeing. Teaching children and adolescents stress management techniques can help them to manage their stress and anxiety, and develop the resilience needed to cope with life's challenges. In this article, we will explore the importance of stress management and provide some strategies for teaching children and adolescents stress management techniques.

Why is Stress Management Important?

Stress management is important for several reasons:

It promotes mental health: When children and adolescents learn how to manage their stress and anxiety, they are better able to maintain good mental health.

It improves physical health: Chronic stress can have a negative impact on physical health. Learning stress management techniques can help children and adolescents to reduce the physical symptoms of stress.

It develops resilience: Learning stress management techniques can help children and adolescents to develop resilience by teaching them how to cope with adversity and challenges.

Strategies for Teaching Stress Management Techniques:

Here are some strategies for teaching stress management techniques to children and adolescents:

Teach deep breathing: Deep breathing is a simple and effective stress management technique that can be practiced anywhere. Encourage children and adolescents to take slow, deep breaths when they feel stressed or anxious.

Practice mindfulness: Mindfulness is a technique that involves focusing on the present moment without judgment. It can help children and adolescents to manage stress and anxiety by teaching them how to stay calm and centered.

Engage in physical activity: Physical activity is a great way to reduce stress and anxiety. Encourage children and adolescents to engage in regular exercise or participate in team sports.

Teach time-management skills: Poor time management can contribute to stress and anxiety. Teach children and adolescents how to manage their time effectively by setting priorities, creating schedules, and avoiding procrastination.

Provide emotional support: Provide emotional support to children and adolescents who are experiencing stress and anxiety. Offer encouragement and help them to develop positive coping strategies.

Teaching stress management techniques to children and adolescents is an important part of promoting resilience. By teaching deep breathing, mindfulness, physical activity, time-management skills, and providing emotional support, you can help children and adolescents to manage their stress and anxiety, and develop the resilience needed to cope with life's challenges. When children and adolescents learn stress management techniques, they are better able to maintain good mental and physical health, and become more resilient and capable of handling adversity.

Scenario 13

***

A 12-year-old boy named Alex is having a difficult time managing his stress and anxiety. He has been struggling with schoolwork and has been feeling overwhelmed with the amount of homework he has been assigned. Alex often feels anxious and worried about not being able to complete his assignments on time.

Alex's teacher notices that he has been struggling and recommends that he participate in a stress management program offered at his school. The program teaches children and adolescents different techniques for managing stress and anxiety, such as deep breathing, progressive muscle relaxation, and meditation.

At first, Alex is hesitant to participate in the program, but he decides to give it a try. In the program, he learns different techniques for managing his stress and anxiety. One technique he finds particularly helpful is deep breathing. He practices taking deep breaths when he feels anxious or overwhelmed, and he finds that it helps him to feel more relaxed and focused.

Another technique Alex learns is progressive muscle relaxation, where he systematically tenses and relaxes different muscle groups in his body. This technique helps him to release tension and feel more relaxed.

Finally, Alex is introduced to meditation. He learns different meditation techniques and practices them regularly at home. Meditation helps him to quiet his mind and focus on the present moment, reducing his feelings of stress and anxiety.

***

Mindfulness and meditation

Mindfulness and meditation are two powerful techniques that can help children and adolescents to develop self-awareness and emotional regulation skills. These techniques are increasingly being used in schools and homes to support children's mental health and well-being. In this article, we will explore the benefits of mindfulness and meditation for children and adolescents, and provide some tips for incorporating these practices into their daily lives.

Benefits of Mindfulness and Meditation:

Improves focus and attention: Practicing mindfulness and meditation can help children and adolescents to improve their focus and attention. This can be particularly helpful for students who struggle with attention deficit hyperactivity disorder (ADHD) or other attention-related difficulties.

Reduces stress and anxiety: Mindfulness and meditation can help children and adolescents to manage stress and anxiety. By focusing on the present moment and cultivating a sense of calm, children and adolescents can learn to regulate their emotions and reduce feelings of stress and anxiety.

Develops self-awareness: Mindfulness and meditation can help children and adolescents to develop self-awareness. By learning to observe their thoughts and emotions without judgment, children and adolescents can become more aware of their internal experiences and better able to regulate their emotions.

Improves emotional regulation: Practicing mindfulness and meditation can help children and adolescents to develop emotional regulation skills. By learning to identify and accept their emotions, children and adolescents can learn to manage their emotional responses more effectively.

Enhances empathy and compassion: Mindfulness and meditation can help children and adolescents to develop empathy and compassion for themselves and others. By cultivating a sense of kindness and compassion, children and adolescents can become more connected to others and more resilient in the face of adversity.

Tips for Incorporating Mindfulness and Meditation into Children's Lives:

Start small: Encourage children and adolescents to start with just a few minutes of mindfulness or meditation each day. Gradually increase the amount of time as they become more comfortable with the practice.

Make it fun: Incorporate mindfulness and meditation into activities that children already enjoy, such as coloring or listening to music. This can make the practice more enjoyable and engaging for children and adolescents.

Use guided meditations: Guided meditations can be particularly helpful for children and adolescents who are new to mindfulness and meditation. There are many apps and websites that offer free guided meditations for children and adolescents.

Practice together: Practicing mindfulness and meditation together as a family can be a great way to make it a regular part of children's lives. Set aside a specific time each day to practice together.

Be patient: It takes time to develop mindfulness and meditation skills. Encourage children and adolescents to be patient and persistent, and to focus on the process rather than the outcome.

Mindfulness and meditation are powerful techniques that can help children and adolescents to develop self-awareness and emotional regulation skills. By improving focus and attention, reducing stress and anxiety, developing self-awareness, improving emotional regulation, and enhancing empathy and compassion, mindfulness and meditation can support children's mental health and wellbeing. Incorporating these practices into children's daily lives can be done in small, fun and gradual ways, including guided meditations, family practice and being patient with progress.

Scenario 14

* * *

Sara is a 14-year-old high school student who is feeling over-whelmed and stressed due to her upcoming exams. She is having trouble concentrating on her studies and is constantly worrying about her performance.

Sara's teacher recommends that she try practicing mindfulness and meditation to help her cope with her stress and anxiety. Sara is initially skeptical but decides to give it a try.

She starts by practicing mindfulness during her study breaks, taking a few deep breaths and focusing her attention on the present moment. She also starts a daily meditation practice, starting with just a few minutes each day and gradually working up to longer sessions.

Over time, Sara notices that she is better able to manage her stress and anxiety. She feels more calm and focused during her studies and is better able to prioritize her tasks. She also finds that she is sleeping better and has more energy during the day.

Sara is grateful for the mindfulness and meditation practices that have helped her to develop greater self-awareness and emotional regulation skills. She continues to practice regularly and shares her newfound knowledge and skills with her friends and family.

* * *

| 4 |

Encouraging Growth Mindset

A growth mindset, which emphasizes the importance of effort and persistence in learning, is an important factor in resilience. Strategies for encouraging a growth mindset in children and adolescents include:

Praising effort

Praising children and adolescents for their effort, rather than innate ability, can have a significant impact on their mindset and ultimately their resilience. When children and adolescents are praised for their innate abilities or intelligence, they may begin to believe that their success is determined solely by their natural talents, rather than their effort and hard work. This can lead to a fixed mindset, in which they may be less likely to take on challenges or persevere in the face of difficulty, fearing failure and the potential damage to their perceived innate ability.

On the other hand, praising effort can help children and adolescents to develop a growth mindset, in which they understand that their success is determined by their effort and hard work. When children and adolescents are praised for their effort, they are more likely to view challenges as opportunities for growth and learning, rather than as threats to their innate ability or intelligence. This mindset can help them to be more resilient in the face of adversity, as they are better able to persevere through challenges and setbacks.

It's important to note that praising effort does not mean that we should ignore innate abilities or talents. It's still important to recognize and appreciate the unique strengths and abilities of children and adolescents. However, when we do praise innate abilities, it's helpful to frame it in a way that emphasizes the effort and hard work that went into developing and honing those abilities.

For example, instead of saying "You're so smart!" after a child performs well on a test, we can say "You worked really hard on that test and it paid off!" This type of praise acknowledges the effort and hard work that went into achieving the positive outcome, rather than just the innate ability.

In addition to praising effort, it's also important to provide constructive feedback that encourages continued effort and growth. For example, if a child or adolescent struggles with a task or assignment, instead of giving up or feeling discouraged, we can provide feedback that helps them identify areas where they can improve and encourages them to keep trying.

Overall, praising effort over innate ability can help children and adolescents to develop a growth mindset, which can have a positive impact on their resilience. When they believe that their success is determined by their effort and hard work, rather than just their natural talents, they are more likely to persevere through challenges and setbacks, and to view those challenges as opportunities for growth and learning.

Scenario 15

* * *

Sarah is a 12-year-old student who is struggling in her math class.

She often becomes frustrated and gives up when she can't solve a problem. One day, her teacher notices that Sarah has been putting in extra effort to understand the material and is making progress, even if it's slow. The teacher decides to praise Sarah for her hard work and determination, saying "I'm proud of you for putting in so much effort to understand these concepts. Keep up the good work!"

Hearing this praise makes Sarah feel encouraged and validated. She realizes that her hard work is paying off, and that she can continue to improve with more effort. She starts to approach math problems with a more positive attitude and a willingness to keep trying, even when things get difficult.

If the teacher had instead praised Sarah for her innate ability in math, saying "You're so smart, you should be able to figure this out easily," Sarah may have felt pressure to live up to the expectation of being naturally good at math. This could have made her feel even more frustrated and discouraged when she struggled with a problem, believing that if she were truly smart, it would come easily to her.

By praising Sarah's effort, her teacher helped her to develop a growth mindset, which emphasizes that intelligence and abilities can be developed through hard work and dedication. This mindset can help Sarah to persist through challenges and see herself as capable of improvement, even in areas where she may struggle initially.

***

Emphasizing learning

Emphasizing the importance of learning, rather than performance, can be a powerful tool for fostering resilience in children and adolescents. When we prioritize learning over performance, we send the message that mistakes and setbacks are a natural part of the learning process, rather than something to be feared or avoided.

In a performance-oriented culture, children and adolescents are often taught to focus on achieving good grades, winning awards, and getting into top schools. While these goals are certainly important, they can also create a sense of pressure and anxiety, as children and adolescents feel that their worth is tied to their achievements.

In contrast, when we emphasize learning, we encourage children and adolescents to focus on the process of acquiring knowledge and skills, rather than just the end result. We help them to see that making mistakes and facing challenges are an essential part of the learning process, and that they can use these experiences as opportunities for growth and improvement.

This emphasis on learning can help children and adolescents to develop a growth mindset, in which they believe that their intelligence and abilities can be developed through hard work and persistence. When they see themselves as learners, rather than performers, they are more likely to take on challenges and persevere in the face of setbacks. They are also more likely to seek out opportunities for learning and growth, rather than avoiding challenges for fear of failure.

Here are some strategies for emphasizing learning over performance: Encourage curiosity and exploration: Encourage children and adolescents to ask questions, explore new topics, and try new things. Help them to see the value of learning for its own sake, rather than just for the sake of achieving a certain outcome.

Focus on effort and progress: Instead of just focusing on grades or test scores, pay attention to the effort and progress that children and adolescents are making. Provide feedback that encourages them to continue working hard and making progress, even if they don't achieve a perfect score or outcome.

Normalize mistakes and setbacks: Help children and adolescents to see that mistakes and setbacks are a natural part of the learning process. Encourage them to reflect on what they've learned from these experiences and how they can apply that knowledge in the future.

Provide opportunities for reflection and self-assessment: Encourage children and adolescents to reflect on their learning process, including their strengths and weaknesses, and to set goals for themselves based on what they want to learn and achieve.

By emphasizing the importance of learning, rather than just performance, we can help children and adolescents to develop a growth mindset that promotes resilience and fosters a love of learning.

Scenario 16

* * *

Imagine a 10-year-old student named Alex who is struggling with his math assignments. He often feels frustrated and discouraged, and he believes that he simply isn't good at math.

However, Alex's teacher emphasizes the importance of learning and growth, rather than simply achieving good grades. She encourages Alex to focus on the process of learning, rather than just the outcome. Alex's teacher provides him with resources and support to improve his math skills, and she praises him for his effort and persistence, rather than his innate ability. She helps Alex to see that everyone struggles with something at some point, and that making mistakes is a natural part of the learning process.

Over time, Alex begins to develop a growth mindset. He starts to see math as a challenge that he can overcome with effort and practice, rather than a subject that he simply isn't good at. He becomes more willing to take risks and make mistakes, and he feels more confident in his ability to learn and grow.

* * *

Encouraging mistakes

Encouraging children and adolescents to embrace mistakes and learn from them is an important aspect of developing resilience. Often, children and adolescents are taught to avoid making mistakes or to feel ashamed when they do make mistakes. However, mistakes can be valuable learning opportunities and can help to build resilience.

When children and adolescents are encouraged to make mistakes, they may feel more comfortable taking risks and trying new things. This can help them to develop a growth mindset and a sense of resilience. Instead of feeling discouraged or defeated when they make a mistake, they can learn from the experience and use it as an opportunity for growth.

One way to encourage mistakes is to normalize them. Let children and adolescents know that everyone makes mistakes and that it is a natural part of the learning process. Encourage them to share their mistakes and what they learned from them with others. This can help to create a culture of learning and growth.

Another way to encourage mistakes is to focus on the process, rather than the outcome. Instead of placing all the emphasis on achieving a particular goal, focus on the steps taken to reach that goal. Emphasize the importance of effort, persistence, and problem-solving skills in achieving success. This can help children and adolescents to see the value in the journey and the learning that comes with it, rather than just the end result.

It is also important to provide a supportive environment for children and adolescents to make mistakes. Encourage them to take risks, but also be there to provide emotional support and guidance when things don't go as planned. Help them to understand that mistakes are a normal part of the learning process and that they can bounce back and try again.

In addition, it is important to model the behavior we want to see in children and adolescents. As adults, we can demonstrate resilience by acknowledging and learning from our own mistakes. By modeling a growth mindset and a willingness to make mistakes, we can encourage children and adolescents to do the same.

Overall, encouraging mistakes is an important part of fostering resilience in children and adolescents. By normalizing mistakes, focusing on the process, providing a supportive environment, and modeling resilience ourselves, we can help children and adolescents to embrace mistakes as opportunities for growth and learning.

Scenario 17

* * *

Sarah is a high school student who struggles with math. She often becomes frustrated and anxious when she can't solve a problem, and she's worried about failing her math class. Her teacher, Mr. Johnson, knows that Sarah has potential but needs to develop a growth mindset to overcome her challenges.

During a recent math class, Mr. Johnson introduced the concept of embracing mistakes as a learning opportunity. He explained that making mistakes is a natural part of the learning process and that it's important to learn from them instead of being discouraged by them.

To put this into practice, Mr. Johnson assigned a challenging math problem that he knew most students would struggle with. When Sarah didn't get the right answer, he encouraged her to keep trying and told her that it's okay to make mistakes. He asked her to think about what she learned from the process and how she could apply it to future problems.

Over time, Sarah began to see her mistakes as an opportunity to learn and improve. She became more comfortable taking risks and trying new approaches, knowing that mistakes were part of the process. She even began to enjoy math and developed a sense of pride in her ability to overcome challenges.

Through Mr. Johnson's encouragement and guidance, Sarah developed resilience and a growth mindset that will serve her well beyond math class.

* * *

Setting challenging goals

Setting challenging goals is an important way to help children and adolescents develop resilience. When young people are encouraged to set goals that are difficult but achievable, they learn to push themselves beyond their comfort zones and to persevere in the face of obstacles.

This can lead to a greater sense of self-efficacy and confidence, both of which are essential components of resilience.

However, it's important to remember that not all goals are created equal. When setting goals for children and adolescents, it's important to strike a balance between challenge and achievability. Goals that are too easy may not provide enough of a challenge to build resilience, while goals that are too difficult may be discouraging and lead to feelings of defeat.

Here are some tips for setting challenging but achievable goals for children and adolescents:

Start small: Begin by setting smaller goals that can be achieved relatively quickly. This can help build momentum and create a sense of accomplishment, which can motivate young people to set more challenging goals in the future.

Make goals specific and measurable: Help young people to articulate their goals in clear, specific terms, and identify measurable outcomes. This can help them to focus their efforts and track their progress.

Provide support and resources: Offer support and resources to help young people achieve their goals. This may include providing coaching or mentoring, offering access to educational resources or materials, or connecting young people with relevant networks or communities.

Celebrate progress: Celebrate progress along the way, even if the ultimate goal has not yet been achieved. Recognizing the effort and commitment that young people put into their goals can help to reinforce the value of perseverance and effort.

Encourage reflection: Encourage young people to reflect on their progress and to identify areas for improvement. This can help them to learn from their experiences and to set more challenging goals in the future.

By setting challenging but achievable goals, children and adolescents can develop a growth mindset and a sense of mastery that can help them to build resilience in the face of adversity.

Scenario 17

* * *

Samantha is a 14-year-old girl who loves playing the guitar. She has been taking guitar lessons for a year and has made good progress, but she feels like she has hit a plateau in her learning. She feels frustrated and unmotivated, and has considered quitting altogether.

Samantha's guitar teacher notices her lack of motivation and suggests that they set a challenging goal together. He asks Samantha to think about a difficult song she would like to learn and they agree to work on it together over the next few months.

At first, Samantha feels overwhelmed by the challenge, but with her teacher's guidance and support, she begins to make progress. She practices every day, sometimes for hours at a time, and begins to see improvements in her playing.

As she gets closer to mastering the song, Samantha feels a sense of accomplishment and pride in herself. She realizes that she is capable of achieving difficult goals with hard work and determination.

Through this experience, Samantha develops a growth mindset and a sense of competence and mastery. She continues to set challenging goals for herself in her guitar playing and in other areas of her life, knowing that she can achieve them with effort and perseverance.

* * *

| 5 |

Promoting Self-Efficacy

Self-efficacy, or belief in one's ability to overcome challenges and achieve goals, is an important factor in resilience. Strategies for promoting self-efficacy in children and adolescents include:

Offering opportunities for mastery experiences

Children and adolescents are more likely to develop resilience when they have experiences that allow them to feel competent and capable. One way to promote these feelings is by offering opportunities for mastery experiences. Mastery experiences are activities or tasks that challenge children and adolescents to learn new skills and achieve success through effort and persistence.

These opportunities can take many forms, such as learning a new sport or musical instrument, taking on leadership roles, or participating in community service projects. The key is that the activity is challenging enough to require effort and practice, but not so difficult that it feels impossible to achieve success.

When children and adolescents engage in mastery experiences, they have the opportunity to develop a sense of competence and self-efficacy. They learn that they are capable of learning and achieving new things with effort and persistence, which can help them to approach future challenges with greater confidence and resilience.

It's important to offer a range of opportunities that cater to different interests and skill levels. For example, some children may enjoy sports or physical activities, while others may prefer creative pursuits like art or music. By offering a variety of options, children and adolescents can explore their interests and find activities that they enjoy and feel confident in.

It's also important to provide support and encouragement throughout the process. Children and adolescents may experience frustration or setbacks as they work towards mastery, and it's important to offer guidance and support to help them overcome these challenges. Adults can provide feedback, encouragement, and help children and adolescents set realistic goals to work towards.

Overall, offering opportunities for mastery experiences can be a powerful way to promote resilience in children and adolescents. By helping them to develop a sense of competence and self-efficacy, these experiences can foster confidence, perseverance, and a growth mindset that will serve them well throughout their lives.

Scenario 18

* * *

Samantha is a 12-year-old girl who has always struggled with math. She often feels discouraged and frustrated in her math class because she can't seem to keep up with her peers. However, Samantha's parents enroll her in an after-school math club where she has the opportunity to work on math problems at her own pace and receive individualized support from a math tutor.

At first, Samantha is hesitant to join the math club because she feels embarrassed about her math skills. However, her parents encourage her to give it a try and remind her that it's okay to make mistakes and learn from them.

In the math club, Samantha starts to feel more confident as she works through math problems and receives positive feedback from her tutor. She even starts to enjoy math and looks forward to going to the club each week. As she masters new math skills and concepts, she begins to develop a sense of competence and self-efficacy.

Samantha's experience in the math club shows the importance of offering children and adolescents opportunities for mastery experiences. By providing a supportive environment where Samantha can learn at her own pace and receive individualized support, she is able to develop a sense of competence and mastery in an area where she previously struggled. This sense of mastery can carry over into other areas of her life, helping her to approach new challenges with confidence and resilience.

* * *

Providing positive feedback

Positive feedback is an essential component of building children's and adolescents' self-esteem and confidence in their abilities. When parents, caregivers, teachers, or other trusted adults provide positive feedback, children and adolescents are more likely to feel valued and supported, which can lead to a greater sense of self-worth and self-efficacy.

Positive feedback should be specific and focused on the effort and progress of the child or adolescent rather than the outcome. For example, instead of saying "Good job on getting an A on your test," saying "I'm proud of how hard you studied for your test and how you never gave up even when you faced challenges" emphasizes the effort and perseverance that led to the positive outcome.

It's also important to note that positive feedback should be genuine and sincere. Children and adolescents are perceptive and can easily detect insincere praise. If they feel that they are being praised just for the sake of it, the positive feedback may lose its impact and even back-fire, leading to a lack of trust and engagement.

Providing positive feedback can also help children and adolescents to develop a growth mindset, which emphasizes the importance of effort and persistence in learning. When children and adolescents receive positive feedback for their efforts and progress, they are more likely to view challenges and mistakes as opportunities for growth and learning rather than as indicators of failure or inadequacy.

In addition, positive feedback can also help children and adolescents to develop resilience by providing them with a sense of accomplishment and self-worth. When children and adolescents receive positive feedback, they are more likely to feel confident in their abilities to overcome challenges and persevere in the face of adversity.

Overall, providing positive feedback is an essential component of helping children and adolescents to develop confidence in their abilities and resilience in the face of challenges. By providing specific and genuine feedback focused on effort and progress, adults can help children and adolescents to develop a growth mindset and a greater sense of self-worth and self-efficacy.

Scenario 19

* * *

A student named Sarah has been struggling with her math class for the past few weeks. She has been getting low grades on her tests and assignments, and she is feeling discouraged about her ability to succeed in the class.

One day, after class, her teacher approaches her and says, "Sarah, I've noticed that you've been putting in a lot of effort into your math work lately. Your hard work is paying off and I can see that you're making progress. Keep up the good work."

Sarah feels validated and encouraged by her teacher's positive feedback. She begins to feel more confident in her abilities and continues to work hard in the class. As a result, she begins to see improvement in her grades and feels more motivated to succeed.

The positive feedback from her teacher not only helped to boost her confidence but also helped to reinforce her efforts and encourage her to keep going.

* * *

Modeling resilience

Children and adolescents learn a lot from the adults in their lives, including how to respond to challenges and adversity. By sharing personal stories of overcoming challenges, adults can model resilience and demonstrate to children and adolescents that it is possible to bounce back from difficult situations. This can help children and adolescents to develop a sense of self-efficacy and the belief that they too can overcome challenges.

When sharing personal stories of resilience, it is important to focus on the process of overcoming challenges rather than just the outcome. This can help children and adolescents to understand that resilience is not just about achieving a certain outcome, but about the effort and perseverance required to get there. By emphasizing the process of overcoming challenges, adults can help children and adolescents to develop a growth mindset and the belief that they can learn and grow from difficult experiences.

It is also important to model resilience in everyday life by responding to challenges and adversity in a positive and constructive way. When faced with setbacks or difficulties, adults can demonstrate resilience by staying positive, seeking out support, and focusing on solutions rather than problems. By modeling resilience in this way, adults can help children and adolescents to develop the skills and mindset needed to bounce back from difficult situations.

In addition to sharing personal stories and modeling resilience, adults can also encourage children and adolescents to seek out role models who have demonstrated resilience. This can include historical figures, celebrities, or even friends and family members who have overcome challenges. By learning about the resilience of others, children and adolescents can gain inspiration and insight into how to develop their own resilience.

Overall, modeling resilience is an important way to help children and adolescents develop the skills and mindset needed to overcome challenges and adversity. By sharing personal stories, modeling resilience in everyday life, and encouraging children and adolescents to seek out role models, adults can help to foster a culture of resilience that supports the growth and development of young people.

Scenario 20

***

Meet Sarah, a high school teacher who wants to help her students develop resilience. One day, during a class on personal development, Sarah decides to share a personal story of her own experience with resilience. She tells her students about how she struggled with anxiety during college, and how she had to work hard to learn coping skills and manage her stress.

As Sarah tells her story, she emphasizes the challenges she faced and how she overcame them. She talks about the strategies she used to manage her anxiety, such as mindfulness and exercise, and how she gradually built up her confidence and resilience over time.

After sharing her story, Sarah invites her students to reflect on their own experiences with resilience and to think about the strategies they can use to overcome challenges. She encourages them to share their thoughts and feelings with each other, and to support each other as they work to develop their own resilience.

Through this activity, Sarah models resilience for her students and creates a safe space for them to reflect on their own experiences. By sharing her personal story, she helps her students to see that resilience is something that can be developed and cultivated over time, and that everyone has the ability to overcome challenges and build a stronger sense of self-efficacy.

* * *

Encouraging self-reflection

Encouraging self-reflection is an important aspect of helping children and adolescents develop resilience. Self-reflection involves taking the time to think about one's experiences, strengths, weaknesses, and how they handle challenging situations. This process can help individuals develop a better understanding of themselves and their abilities, which can ultimately lead to increased confidence and resilience.

To encourage self-reflection, adults can provide children and adolescents with opportunities to think about their experiences and share their thoughts and feelings. This can involve asking open-ended questions such as "How did you feel when that happened?" or "What did you learn from that experience?" Adults can also encourage children and adolescents to journal or keep a personal reflection log to help them process their experiences and emotions.

Another way to encourage self-reflection is by providing feedback that encourages critical thinking and self-evaluation. Instead of simply praising or criticizing a child's performance, adults can ask questions that encourage the child to reflect on their efforts and identify areas for improvement. For example, instead of saying "Great job!" after a project, an adult could ask "What did you learn from this project? Is there anything you would do differently next time?"

By encouraging self-reflection, adults can help children and adolescents to develop a deeper understanding of themselves and their abilities. This can lead to increased self-efficacy, which is an important component of resilience. When individuals believe in their ability to handle challenging situations, they are more likely to approach adversity with a positive outlook and a willingness to learn and grow.

Scenario 21

* * *

Imagine a 14-year-old girl named Maya who is struggling with self-confidence and doubts her abilities in school. Maya's teacher notices her struggles and decides to encourage self-reflection by assigning a personal strengths project. The project requires Maya to reflect on her past successes and challenges and identify her personal strengths and areas for growth. Maya spends time reflecting on her experiences and realizes that she is a creative problem-solver and has strong organizational skills. She also realizes that she struggles with time management and procrastination.

After completing the project, Maya feels more confident in her abilities and has a better understanding of her areas for growth. Her teacher praises her for her self-reflection and encourages her to use her strengths to tackle her challenges. Maya feels more empowered to take control of her academic success and is motivated to work on improving her time management skills. Through this process of self-reflection, Maya has developed a sense of self-efficacy and is better equipped to face future challenges.

* * *

| 6 |

Developing Social and Emotional Intelligence

Social and emotional intelligence, or the ability to understand and manage emotions, and navigate social relationships, is an important factor in resilience. Strategies for developing social and emotional intelligence in children and adolescents include:

Teaching emotional literacy

Emotional literacy is an important component of emotional intelligence, which is crucial for developing resilience. Emotional literacy involves the ability to recognize, understand, and express emotions in a healthy and effective way. Children and adolescents who are emotionally literate are better able to manage their emotions and navigate social relationships, which can help them to cope with stress and adversity.

To teach emotional literacy, parents and caregivers can start by helping children and adolescents to identify and label emotions. This can involve using simple and concrete language to describe different emotions, such as happy, sad, angry, or afraid. Encouraging children to express their emotions in healthy and appropriate ways can also help to develop emotional literacy. For example, parents can encourage children to talk about their feelings or express them through art, music, or other creative outlets.

Another important aspect of emotional literacy is developing an understanding of how emotions are connected to behavior. Children and adolescents who are able to identify the emotions underlying their behavior are better equipped to regulate their behavior and make healthy choices. Parents and caregivers can help children to understand this connection by discussing how different emotions can influence behavior and by providing guidance on how to manage emotions in healthy ways.

Teaching children and adolescents to practice empathy and perspective-taking is also an important part of emotional literacy. Empathy involves being able to understand and share the feelings of others, while perspective-taking involves being able to see things from another person's point of view. By practicing empathy and perspective-taking, children and adolescents can develop stronger social relationships and a greater understanding of themselves and others.

Overall, teaching emotional literacy can help children and adolescents to develop emotional intelligence, which is a key factor in resilience. By being able to identify and manage their emotions, as well as understand and empathize with others, children and adolescents can build the social and emotional skills they need to navigate stress and adversity.

Scenario 22

* * *

Meet Sarah, a 10-year-old girl who often feels overwhelmed and frustrated with her schoolwork. When she gets home, she usually ends up crying in her room, feeling like a failure. Her parents are worried about her and don't know how to help.

One day, Sarah's teacher introduces the class to the concept of emotional literacy. She explains how emotions are like different colors on a palette, and just like an artist mixes colors to create new shades, we can learn to identify and understand our emotions. Sarah is intrigued by this idea and decides to learn more about it.

Over the next few weeks, Sarah practices identifying and labeling her emotions, using a chart that her teacher provided. She discovers that when she's feeling overwhelmed with schoolwork, it's not just frustration, but also anxiety and self-doubt. By recognizing and naming these emotions, Sarah begins to feel more in control of her feelings.

With her teacher's guidance, Sarah also learns coping skills, such as deep breathing and positive self-talk, to manage her emotions when they feel overwhelming. She also starts to share her feelings with her parents, who are relieved that she's opening up to them.

As Sarah continues to practice emotional literacy, she becomes more confident and self-aware. She's able to tackle her schoolwork with a new sense of resilience and feels empowered to take charge of her emotions.

In this scenario, teaching emotional literacy helped Sarah to identify and manage her emotions, leading to improved resilience and confidence. It also allowed her to connect more deeply with her parents and feel more supported.

* * *

Practicing empathy

Empathy is the ability to understand and share the feelings of others. Practicing empathy can be an effective way for children and adolescents to develop social intelligence and emotional regulation skills. When children learn to empathize with others, they become better able to communicate and form positive relationships.

To teach empathy to children and adolescents, adults can model empathetic behavior and use age-appropriate materials and activities that focus on emotions and perspective-taking.

Here are some ways adults can encourage children and adolescents to practice empathy:

Acknowledge and validate emotions: When children and adolescents express their emotions, adults can acknowledge and validate their feelings. This can help them to feel heard and understood, and it can also model empathetic behavior.

Use books and stories: Reading books and stories that focus on emotions and perspective-taking can be a helpful way to encourage empathy in children and adolescents. Adults can discuss the characters' emotions and ask children and adolescents to consider how they might feel in similar situations.

Role-play: Role-playing can help children and adolescents to practice empathy and perspective-taking. Adults can provide different scenarios and ask children and adolescents to imagine how they would feel in those situations.

Encourage active listening: Encouraging children and adolescents to listen actively to others can help them to develop empathy. Adults can model active listening behavior by paraphrasing what the speaker has said and asking clarifying questions.

Teach conflict resolution: Teaching conflict resolution skills can help children and adolescents to empathize with others and resolve conflicts in a positive and productive way. Adults can teach children and adolescents to express their feelings and needs assertively and to listen actively to the other person's perspective.

By practicing empathy, children and adolescents can develop social and emotional intelligence, which can help them to build positive relationships and manage stress and adversity.

Scenario 23

* * *

Sara is a 12-year-old girl who has recently started middle school. She has always been shy and finds it difficult to make friends. On her first day of school, she sits alone at lunch and feels left out when she sees other students chatting and laughing together.

One day, during her social studies class, the teacher assigns a group project on a current event. Sara is paired up with two other students, Jack and Maya. Jack is outgoing and confident, while Maya is quiet and reserved like Sara.

As they work on their project, Sara notices that Maya seems upset and is not contributing much to the discussion. Instead of ignoring her, Sara decides to practice empathy and put herself in Maya's shoes. She remembers how lonely she felt on her first day of school and wonders if Maya is feeling the same way.

Sara decides to talk to Maya privately after class and asks her if everything is okay. Maya confides in her that her parents are going through a divorce and she's been feeling really sad lately. Sara listens attentively and offers words of support and encouragement. She also suggests that they work together on the project outside of class so they can get to know each other better.

* * *

Encouraging positive relationships

Encouraging positive relationships with others is an important factor in fostering resilience in children and adolescents. Positive relationships can provide emotional support, a sense of belonging, and opportunities for social learning and growth.

Here are some ways to encourage positive relationships:

Model positive relationship behaviors: Children and adolescents learn by watching the adults in their lives. Modeling positive relationship behaviors, such as empathy, communication, and respect, can help children and adolescents to develop these skills themselves.

Encourage socialization: Encourage children and adolescents to spend time with peers and participate in social activities. This can include extracurricular activities, community events, and social clubs.

Promote open communication: Encourage open communication between children and adolescents and their peers, family members, and teachers. This can help to build trust and strengthen relationships.

Teach conflict resolution skills: Teach children and adolescents how to resolve conflicts in a constructive way, such as through active listening, compromise, and problem-solving.

Foster a sense of community: Encourage children and adolescents to participate in community service and outreach activities. This can help to foster a sense of community and social responsibility.

Address bullying and negative behavior: Address bullying and negative behavior in a proactive and constructive way. Teach children and adolescents how to stand up for themselves and others, and how to recognize and respond to negative behavior.

By encouraging positive relationships, children and adolescents can develop social intelligence and a sense of belonging, which can help to foster resilience in the face of adversity.

Scenario 24

* * *

Samantha is a 13-year-old girl who has recently moved to a new city with her family. She feels lonely and disconnected from her new community, and is struggling to make friends at her new school. Samantha's parents notice that she seems down and isolated, and they decide to take action.

They start by encouraging Samantha to join a local youth group that meets regularly in their neighborhood. At the youth group, Samantha meets other teens her age who share her interests and hobbies. She starts to form friendships and feels a sense of belonging in the group.

Samantha's parents also make an effort to get to know their new neighbors and become more involved in community activities. They attend local events and festivals, and invite other families over for dinner. Samantha is able to meet more people and expand her social circle outside of school.

Over time, Samantha begins to feel more connected and supported by her community. She is happier and more confident, and her grades and academic performance improve. By encouraging positive relationships and social connections, Samantha's parents were able to help her develop a sense of belonging and resilience.

* * *

Developing communication skills

Effective communication is a vital life skill that enables children and adolescents to express themselves and engage with others successfully. Developing communication skills helps them to interact with others, build positive relationships, and avoid misunderstandings. In addition to helping children and adolescents communicate their emotions and needs effectively, developing communication skills can also contribute to their resilience.

Here are some ways to help children and adolescents develop effective communication skills:

Encourage active listening: Active listening involves paying attention to what the other person is saying and responding appropriately. Encouraging children and adolescents to actively listen to others can help them to understand different perspectives and build positive relationships. You can model active listening by giving them your undivided attention when they are speaking to you.

Teach assertiveness: Assertiveness is the ability to express one's needs, feelings, and opinions confidently and respectfully. Teaching children and adolescents to be assertive can help them to communicate their needs and boundaries effectively, which can contribute to their self-esteem and resilience.

Model effective communication: Children and adolescents learn by example, so it is essential to model effective communication in your interactions with them. This includes using "I" statements to express your feelings, speaking respectfully, and actively listening to them.

Use open-ended questions: Using open-ended questions can encourage children and adolescents to express themselves more fully and develop their communication skills. Instead of asking yes or no questions, ask questions that encourage them to elaborate on their thoughts and feelings.

Practice active communication: Practicing active communication involves asking questions, clarifying misunderstandings, and expressing empathy. Encouraging children and adolescents to practice active communication can help them to navigate social situations more effectively and build positive relationships.

Encourage communication in different settings: Encouraging children and adolescents to communicate in different settings can help them to develop their communication skills. This can include participating in group discussions, public speaking, or engaging in social activities.

By developing effective communication skills, children and adolescents can learn to express their emotions and needs effectively, navigate social relationships, and build positive relationships. These skills can contribute to their resilience by enabling them to manage stress and adversity more effectively.

Scenario 25

***

Samantha is a 13-year-old girl who has recently started attending a new school. She's finding it difficult to make friends, and often feels anxious and alone during lunch and recess. Samantha's parents are worried about her and want to help her develop better communication skills so she can make friends and feel more confident in social situations.

They enroll Samantha in a social skills group that focuses on communication. In the group, Samantha learns how to initiate conversations, ask questions, and listen actively. She also practices using assertive communication to express her feelings and needs in a clear and respectful way.

After a few weeks of attending the group, Samantha feels more confident and less anxious in social situations. She starts using her new communication skills to talk to her classmates, and even initiates a conversation with a girl she's never spoken to before. The two of them discover that they have a shared interest in art, and they start eating lunch together and working on art projects during recess.

Through the social skills group, Samantha was able to develop communication skills that helped her to connect with others and build positive relationships.

***

| 7 |

Fostering Resilience in Specific Populations

Certain populations may face unique challenges that require tailored strategies for fostering resilience. Some examples include:

Children and adolescents with disabilities

Children and adolescents with disabilities face unique challenges in developing resilience, as they may experience physical, cognitive, or social barriers that can limit their ability to cope with stress and adversity. However, with the right support and accommodations, children and adolescents with disabilities can develop resilience and thrive.

One important strategy for fostering resilience in children and adolescents with disabilities is to provide accommodations and support services. This may include accommodations in the classroom or at home, such as assistive technology, modified curriculum, or specialized therapies. It may also include support services such as counseling or mentoring, which can help children and adolescents with disabilities to develop coping skills and self-efficacy.

Another important strategy is to emphasize strengths and abilities rather than limitations. Children and adolescents with disabilities may be accustomed to hearing negative messages about their abilities, which can undermine their confidence and resilience. By emphasizing their strengths and accomplishments, and providing opportunities for success, adults can help children and adolescents with disabilities to develop a positive sense of self and a belief in their ability to overcome challenges.

In addition to these strategies, it is important to recognize that resilience in children and adolescents with disabilities is often influenced by broader social and cultural factors. For example, children and adolescents with disabilities may face discrimination or exclusion from social activities or employment opportunities. Addressing these barriers and promoting social inclusion can help to foster resilience and improve outcomes for children and adolescents with disabilities.

Ultimately, fostering resilience in children and adolescents with disabilities requires a holistic approach that addresses their unique needs and strengths, as well as broader societal factors that can impact their well-being. By providing support, emphasizing strengths, and promoting social inclusion, adults can help children and adolescents with disabilities to develop resilience and thrive.

Scenario 26

* * *

John is a 12-year-old boy with dyslexia who has struggled with reading and writing since he started school. Despite his efforts, he has consistently performed below grade level and has received negative feedback from his teachers and classmates. As a result, John has developed low self-esteem and is reluctant to try new things or take risks.

Recognizing John's challenges, his parents and teachers have implemented a number of strategies to foster his resilience. First, they have provided accommodations in the classroom, such as extra time for assignments and access to assistive technology. They have also connected John with a reading tutor who specializes in dyslexia, and a therapist who helps him develop coping strategies for managing stress and negative emotions.

To further support John's resilience, his parents and teachers have made a concerted effort to emphasize his strengths and abilities. They have praised his creativity, problem-solving skills, and sense of humor, and have encouraged him to pursue his interests in art and music. They have also provided opportunities for John to succeed and develop a sense of mastery, such as by allowing him to create artwork for classroom projects or perform in the school talent show.

Finally, John's parents and teachers have recognized the importance of addressing broader social and cultural factors that may impact his resilience. They have advocated for his rights as a student with a disability, and have worked to promote social inclusion by encouraging his participation in extracurricular activities and community events.

Over time, these strategies have helped John to develop resilience and confidence in his abilities. He now approaches challenges with a growth mindset and is willing to try new things, even if they are difficult. By providing the right support and emphasizing his strengths, John's parents and teachers have helped him to thrive despite his learning differences.

* * *

Children and adolescents from low-income families

Children and adolescents from low-income families often face unique challenges that can impact their ability to develop resilience. However, there are strategies that can be implemented to support their development of resilience.

One strategy is to provide access to resources and support services. This can include access to healthcare, nutritious food, safe housing, and educational opportunities. Organizations that provide support services such as afterschool programs, mentorship programs, and job training programs can also be beneficial for children and adolescents from low-income families. These resources can help to alleviate stressors and provide opportunities for growth and development.

Another strategy is to emphasize the importance of education and future planning. Children and adolescents from low-income families may face additional barriers to academic success, such as lack of access to resources like textbooks, technology, and tutoring. Emphasizing the importance of education and providing additional resources and support for academic success can help these individuals to develop a sense of purpose and direction for their future.

In addition, it is important to recognize and value the strengths and abilities of children and adolescents from low-income families, rather than focusing solely on their limitations. By emphasizing their strengths and abilities, and providing opportunities for them to showcase these strengths, individuals from low-income families can develop a sense of pride and confidence in themselves.

Overall, by providing access to resources and support services, emphasizing the importance of education and future planning, and recognizing and valuing strengths and abilities, children and adolescents from low-income families can develop resilience and overcome the challenges they face.

Senerio 27

* * *

Samantha is a 14-year-old girl from a low-income family. She lives in a small apartment with her parents and two younger siblings. Her father works long hours as a janitor and her mother cleans houses to make ends meet. Samantha often feels stressed and overwhelmed by her family's financial situation, which makes it difficult for her to focus on her schoolwork.

To help Samantha build resilience, her school offers a program called "College Bound," which provides resources and support for students from low-income families who are interested in pursuing higher education. Samantha decides to join the program and meets with her mentor, who is a college student from a similar background.

Through the program, Samantha has access to tutoring, college preparation workshops, and financial aid resources. She also participates in college campus visits and meets other students who are also interested in higher education.

The program helps Samantha to see that her family's financial situation does not have to determine her future. She becomes more motivated to do well in school and starts to develop a sense of hope for her future. With the support of her mentor and the program, Samantha feels more confident in her ability to succeed and thrive, despite the challenges she faces.

* * *

Children and adolescents who have experienced trauma

Children and adolescents who have experienced trauma can benefit from a range of strategies to foster resilience. One important approach is to provide access to trauma-focused therapy and support services, such as counseling, group therapy, or peer support groups. These resources can help children and adolescents to process their experiences, learn coping skills, and develop a sense of safety and security.

It is also important to promote a sense of safety and security in the child or adolescent's environment. This can involve creating a stable and supportive home environment, providing consistent routines and expectations, and ensuring access to basic needs such as food, clothing, and shelter.

In addition, it can be helpful to support the child or adolescent in building positive relationships with caring and supportive adults, such as teachers, mentors, or family members. This can involve providing opportunities for the child or adolescent to engage in positive activities, such as sports or clubs, where they can interact with supportive peers and role models.

Finally, it is important to promote a sense of empowerment and self-efficacy in the child or adolescent. This can involve helping them to identify and develop their strengths and interests, and providing opportunities for them to practice problem-solving and decision-making skills. It can also involve helping them to identify and challenge negative beliefs or self-talk that may be hindering their ability to cope with stress and adversity.

Overall, fostering resilience in children and adolescents who have experienced trauma requires a comprehensive and collaborative approach that addresses their physical, emotional, and social needs, and provides them with the support and resources necessary to thrive.

Scenario 28

***

Imagine a 12-year-old child who has experienced multiple traumatic events, including physical and emotional abuse by a family member, witnessing domestic violence, and living in poverty. The child has been struggling with symptoms of anxiety, depression, and post-traumatic stress disorder (PTSD), including nightmares, flashbacks, and hypervigilance.

To foster resilience in this child, it is essential to provide trauma-focused therapy and support services. The child could receive counseling from a licensed therapist trained in trauma-focused cognitive behavioral therapy (TF-CBT), which is an evidence-based treatment for children and adolescents who have experienced trauma. The therapist can help the child process their traumatic experiences and develop coping skills to manage their symptoms.

In addition to therapy, it is crucial to promote a sense of safety and security for the child. This could involve ensuring that the child has a stable and safe living environment, free from abuse and neglect. It could also involve providing the child with basic needs such as food, clothing, and shelter.

Moreover, the child could benefit from participating in activities that promote positive relationships with peers and adults, such as after-school programs or community-based programs like sports teams or clubs. These activities can help the child develop social connections and a sense of belonging.

Overall, it is essential to provide a comprehensive approach to support the child's resilience, including trauma-focused therapy, safety and security, and positive relationships and activities. With the right support, the child can build resilience and overcome the traumatic experiences they have faced.

* * *

| 8 |

Building Resilience Through Community and School-Based Interventions

Community and school-based interventions can play an important role in building resilience in children and adolescents. Some examples of interventions that have been shown to be effective include:

Mentoring programs

Mentoring programs are a valuable tool for fostering resilience in children and adolescents. Mentors can provide young people with positive role models and supportive relationships that can help them to develop a sense of belonging, self-efficacy, and social intelligence.

Mentoring programs typically involve pairing a young person with a trained adult mentor who can offer guidance, support, and encouragement. Mentors may meet with their mentees regularly, providing a safe and supportive space for young people to discuss their challenges, goals, and aspirations. These programs may also include group activities and events that allow mentees to connect with their peers and develop social skills.

One of the key benefits of mentoring programs is that they can provide young people with positive role models. Mentors can serve as examples of resilience, perseverance, and success, inspiring young people to believe in their own potential. By sharing their own stories of overcoming challenges, mentors can help mentees to develop a growth mindset and a sense of self-efficacy.

Mentoring programs can also offer young people a supportive relationship that may not be available to them elsewhere. Many children and adolescents lack positive adult role models in their lives, and may feel isolated or unsupported. A mentor can provide a listening ear, emotional support, and practical guidance, helping young people to feel more connected and less alone.

In addition to offering emotional support, mentoring programs can also help young people to develop social intelligence. Mentees may have the opportunity to interact with their mentor's network of friends and colleagues, and to participate in group activities that promote teamwork and communication skills. This can be especially beneficial for young people who may have limited social opportunities or who struggle with social skills.

Mentoring programs can be particularly beneficial for children and adolescents who face additional challenges, such as those from low-income families or those who have experienced trauma. Mentors can provide a source of stability and consistency in the lives of young people who may be facing difficult circumstances. They can also serve as advocates, helping mentees to access resources and support services that can help them to overcome barriers and achieve their goals.

In summary, mentoring programs are a valuable tool for fostering resilience in children and adolescents. By providing positive role models, supportive relationships, and opportunities for social and emotional development, mentors can help young people to develop the skills and strengths they need to overcome challenges and thrive.

Social and emotional learning programs

Social and emotional learning (SEL) programs are designed to promote the development of essential social and emotional skills in children and adolescents. These programs provide young people with the tools they need to navigate social relationships, regulate their emotions, and cope with stress and adversity.

One of the key benefits of SEL programs is that they teach children and adolescents coping skills that they can use throughout their lives. By learning to manage their emotions and stress in healthy ways, young people can reduce their risk of developing mental health problems and improve their overall well-being.

SEL programs typically include a variety of activities and exercises that are designed to promote the development of specific skills. For example, students may participate in role-playing exercises to practice effective communication skills, or learn relaxation techniques such as deep breathing and visualization to manage stress.

Another important aspect of SEL programs is the emphasis on emotional regulation. By learning to identify and regulate their emotions, young people can better manage challenging situations and reduce their risk of developing mental health problems such as anxiety and depression.

In addition to coping skills and emotional regulation, SEL programs also focus on developing social skills. Through group activities and discussions, students learn to build positive relationships, resolve conflicts, and work effectively in teams.

SEL programs have been shown to be effective in improving a wide range of outcomes for children and adolescents. Research has demonstrated that these programs can lead to improvements in academic performance, social skills, and mental health. In addition, studies have shown that SEL programs can reduce problem behaviors such as aggression and substance use.

Overall, social and emotional learning programs can play an important role in promoting resilience in children and adolescents. By providing young people with the skills they need to cope with stress and adversity, these programs can help to improve their overall well-being and set them on a path to success.

After-school programs

After-school programs can play an important role in promoting resilience in children and adolescents by providing them with opportunities for positive experiences and relationships. These programs can provide a safe and structured environment for youth during out-of-school hours, which can reduce the risk of engaging in risky behaviors or experiencing negative outcomes.

One key benefit of after-school programs is that they offer opportunities for mastery experiences. These experiences involve engaging in activities or tasks that are challenging but achievable, and can help youth develop a sense of competence and confidence in their abilities. After-school programs may offer a variety of activities, such as sports, arts and crafts, academic enrichment, and community service, that allow youth to explore their interests and develop new skills.

In addition to providing opportunities for mastery experiences, after-school programs can also foster positive relationships with peers and adults. Building supportive relationships is an important factor in resilience, as it can provide youth with a sense of belonging, support, and encouragement. After-school programs can offer a space where youth can interact with peers who share their interests and make new friends. Adults in after-school programs can also serve as positive role models and mentors, providing guidance and support to youth.

After-school programs can also provide a structure and routine for youth, which can be particularly important for those who may not have consistent structure or support at home. By offering a safe and predictable environment, after-school programs can help youth feel more secure and less stressed. This can be particularly beneficial for children and adolescents who have experienced trauma or who come from low-income families.

Overall, after-school programs can play a vital role in promoting resilience in children and adolescents by providing opportunities for mastery experiences, positive relationships with peers and adults, and a structured and supportive environment. These programs can be particularly beneficial for youth who may face challenges or adversity in their lives, and can help to support their emotional, social, and academic development.

Community-based programs

Community-based programs, such as sports teams, clubs, and volunteer organizations, can provide children and adolescents with opportunities for social connection and positive relationships with peers and adults outside of their immediate family and school environment.

Participating in community-based programs can also help children and adolescents to develop skills and strengths, such as leadership, teamwork, and problem-solving, that can contribute to their overall sense of resilience. These programs can also provide a sense of purpose and meaning, as well as a sense of belonging to a larger community.

Community-based programs can be particularly beneficial for children and adolescents who may not have access to other resources or opportunities for positive social and emotional development. For example, children and adolescents from low-income families or those who live in underserved communities may not have access to extracurricular activities or other resources that can contribute to their overall well-being.

Some examples of community-based programs include:

Youth sports teams: Participating in youth sports teams can provide children and adolescents with opportunities for physical activity, skill-building, and teamwork. In addition to promoting physical health, sports teams can also promote social connections and positive relationships with coaches and teammates.

Volunteer organizations: Participating in volunteer organizations, such as a local food bank or animal shelter, can provide children and adolescents with opportunities to give back to their community and develop a sense of purpose and meaning. Volunteer work can also promote empathy and social responsibility.

Youth groups and clubs: Joining a youth group or club, such as a scouting organization or theater group, can provide children and adolescents with opportunities to develop skills and interests outside of the school environment. These groups can also promote positive relationships with peers and adult mentors.

Overall, community-based programs can provide children and adolescents with important opportunities for social connection, skill-building, and personal growth. These programs can also contribute to their overall sense of resilience and well-being, particularly for those who may not have access to other resources or opportunities.

In conclusion, cultivating resilience in children and adolescents is essential for their emotional and psychological well-being. This book has provided practical strategies for fostering resilience in children and adolescents. By building positive relationships, teaching coping skills, encouraging growth mindset, promoting self-efficacy, developing social and emotional intelligence, and addressing specific populations and challenges, caregivers and educators can help children and adolescents navigate life's challenges with greater ease.

David Olubiyi is a passionate author dedicated to empowering individuals with the knowledge and tools to thrive in their lives. David's interest lies in the areas of resilience, positive psychology, and personal development. Through his insightful writings, he aims to inspire readers to tap into their inner strength, overcome challenges, and lead fulfilling lives. David's engaging writing style and practical approach make his works accessible to a wide range of audiences. He is committed to making a positive impact on individuals' well-being and is actively involved in promoting resilience in children and adolescents.

.

www.ingramcontent.com/pod-product-compliance
Lightning Source LLC
Chambersburg PA
CBHW040856120626

46551CB00001B/39